AUTHENTIC AMISH COOKING SERIES

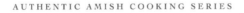

Amish Quilting
Cookbook

Quilts. Cooking. Experience both as 58 Amish quilters
share 316 of their best dishes and finest quilts.

Star Spin © Barbara Schaffeld, Vale, OR 97918

Pineapple Delight © 1989 Linda Parker, Agent, San Marlos, CA 92069

Triple Irish Chain with Star © 1989 Vesta (Ropp) Miller, Millersburg, OH

Apple Basket Quilt Design (gift page) © 2003 Mary Nolt, East Earl, PA

Weaver Fever © 1991 Jackie Robinson, Eureka, MT. Pattern available by
contacting Lone Star Quilt Shop or Animas Quilts Publishing at 406-889-
5501.

For information on quilts, contact
Lone Star Quilts, PO Box 32, Mt. Hope, Ohio 44660

A Stitch in Time Tips on pages 7, 17, 39, 44, 114, 119, and 130
from the *Quilt of Life* by Mary Tatem. Used by kind permission of
Barbour Publishing, Inc., Uhrichsville, Ohio

Quilt photography by Larry McBride
Book design by Virginia Beachy

ISBN 1-890050-73-3

© Copyright September 2003 Carlisle Press

5M0903

Carlisle Press
WALNUT CREEK
2673 TR 421
Sugarcreek, OH 44681

DEDICATION

to women everywhere
who enjoy the fine art of quilting
and the delight of good food.

ACKNOWLEDGMENTS

I want to thank all the quilting ladies who took the time to write their stories and were willing to share their favorite recipes for this book.

Special thanks to our daughters, Barbara, Ada Marie, and Miriam, for their encouragement in getting the book started.

—*Sara Yoder*

TABLE OF CONTENTS

Featured Quilts

INTRODUCTION

We moved to Mt. Hope in 1969 and have lived here for the last 43 years. We started Lone Star Quilt Shop in 1973. It all started when we had a porch sale (my husband, Ervin, has a shoe store) and sold a few pieces of fabric, mostly broadcloth and cotton. As our family grew, (we have three daughters and 4 sons) we added more fabrics. When Ervin decided to build onto his shoe store we decided a quilt shop would be nice to have. I had already pieced and quilted my first quilt, a unique Log Cabin. I sold it to a local quilt shop. At that time the children were small and I had time for one quilt each winter. With time, I moved the fabric store upstairs and began making quilts in the basement of our shop.

It was daughter Barbara's idea to start a quilt shop. So she made her first one, a Nine Patch. Eventually the younger two daughters made their own first quilt, a Nine Patch as well. They sold well, helping the quilt shop off to a good start. Our one daughter has designed original quilts on her own and continues to quilt as time allows.

Six of our children are married. We are blessed with 21 grand-children.

One of our family's quilt-making highlights was making 9 quilts for Governor Celeste. He placed them in his governor's mansion in Columbus, Ohio.

Several years after that, Land's End catalog wanted our quilts. Over the course of eight years, we made hundreds of quilts for Land's End.

Today, with the girls married, we have hired girls to take care of customers, and neighbor women (see Quilters Share on page XII) to help with each step of the quilting process by hand, which is still done the same way it was 30 years ago.

SARA'S DAUGHTERS SHARE

I became interested in quilts at the age of 10. I enjoyed watching my mother and the other ladies piece and sew, and decided to give it a try myself. I pieced my first quilt, aDouble Nine Patch, when I was 13.

When I finished my schooling at Mt. Hope Elementary, I started working in the family quilt shop beside our home on the south edge of Mt. Hope, Ohio. My mother had me piece Christms stockings that were sold in the Land's End catalog.

Today I spend much of my time looking after our five children. I also help out my husband, Ernie, in our business, Homestead Furniture, located north of Mt. Hope. Although I don't have much time for quilting, I enjoy sewing most of the clothing for our family.

Barbara Ann Hershberger

A t school age I stood by Mom's side, watching as she cut and pieced quilts. At the age of fourteen, she wanted me to start piecing quilts, so we picked out some of her fabrics and started to cut and piece a Nine Patch quilt. It turned out well and I began to like it, and made more difficult and complicated quilts that were more challenging.

Mom and I started designing some quilts of our own by now, and I designed several of my own — Peace at the Ocean, Grandma's Fancy Star, and more.

I'm married and have six children, and I still piece quilts when time permits me and love to sew them.

Sew long,

Ada Marie Miller

I 'm a daughter of Ervin and Sara Yoder and began helping Mother in the quilt shop at 12 years old. As a grew older, Mother started me on the Nine Patch quilt, of which I made many. I also enjoyed taking care of customers. I remember all the work we put into making quilts for Land's End. After I got married, I continued to piece quilts, many of which are in this book. We have four children, and I love to sew for my family.

Miriam Swartzentruber

QUILTERS SHARE

*Meet seven of the quilters that work to make the quilts in this book
the masterpieces they are. These women work out of their home as
a long distance assembly line, each doing their part in turn, and
all doing it by hand.*

I have been marking quilts for Lone Star Quilt Shop for more than 20 years. I remember the first one that I marked was either an Alabama Star or a Lone Star. With the many stencils that are available now, it is a lot faster and easier than it was when I started.

In December of 1984 I had an accident with a gasoline light, and 60% of my body was burned. I was in the Akron Children's Burn Center for three weeks, then back for more skin grafting several times and for therapy for most of a year. Sewing and quilt marking were two of the things that I could do soon after I got out of the hospital. I have also marked lots of plain quilts for other ladies besides the pieced ones for Lone Star. My sister, Verna Weaver, also helps with marking when things get piled up. —*Clara Yoder, Quilt Marker*

Mom started quilting for Sara Yoder around 1985. We had put up new buildings a little back from John's parents, off the home farm. The children were small yet, the youngest nearly two at that time, and Mom enjoyed quilting, so she started that to help with the family income. We also milked 9-10 cows and sent the milk to Kidron Dairy.

There were four children, one boy and three girls. Edna, the oldest daughter began quilting when she was 12 years old.

Susie, the youngest, used to wish she could also quilt, sometimes she'd take a straight pin and a rocking chair cushion and pretended to be quilting! And she also remembers how it was to be sick and having to stay at home from school, lying on the lounge with everything quiet, except Mom pulling her thread through the quilt and the quilt frame creaking.

Katie was twelve, and Susie eleven, when they began quilting. One of their first days of quilting, Mom and Edna went away for the day, then Katie and Susie quilted one side the small border, which had a twist marked on it. That kept them busy to get it done before they came home!

We have our differences in what kinds of quilts we like. Mom enjoys quilting marked off feathers, while some of the girls would rather quilt a quarter inch away from the seams. Appliquéd quilts aren't too bad. It's always interesting if we get a new kind of quilt. Of course, we like the ones best that are soft and easy stitching! It also helps if the colors match. We think Sara seems to know what colors belong together for a good-looking quilt.

By now the three oldest children are 21 and over, the youngest is 19. Edna taught school for two terms, but at this time she's mostly working away as a hired girl at different places. The two other girls also have their turns for being someone's hired girl. But at home there's usually a quilt in frame!

—*Mrs. John M. Zook and daughters Edna, Katie, and Susie*

I can't really remember how old I was, but I think around 13 or 14. My mom used to quilt for an English lady from Cleveland. First I just took a pin and tried to find out how to use a thimble, but it wasn't long until I got the hang of it. After I got married I wanted to something other than just housework, so I decided to quilt, which was a nice little income besides what we made in our harness shop. When my daughters were in 7th and 8th grade, they too wanted to learn how to do it, and soon they helped me quite a bit. After we did one Alabama Star after another they sometimes grew very tired of it, so we made a deadline to quit, no longer than 8:30 in the evening, which I, too, enjoyed. We often sang all evening while quilting. I made quilts for our five children now, four of which are married, and the girls also quilted some in their spare time. It's still very interesting to get together and quilt for a day.

—*Sevilla Swartzentruber, Quilter*

I n my younger years I taught myself to embroider on scarves and pillowcases. Later I did three state bird quilts for my children. Then I also went to our monthly sewing and got the desire to quilt. That desire has stayed with me ever since. About 17 years ago, Sara gave my sister a rose quilt to be appliquéd and she turned it over to me. It was my first one and I continued when Sara had some appliquéing to do. I still have the picture of that first quilt. I then appliquéd some blocks of my own to quilt. I wish I would have counted the quilts over these years. I am slowing down since I'm 82 years old.   —*Lucinda Yoder, Appliqué*

A few lines on how Mom got started quilting. She was at the age of 12 when her mother had her take the needles without a knotted thread and quilt on a quilt that was just for family use and pulled thread on through until her stitches looked nice enough to leave in. Then she made a knot on the end. It took her a good month to learn how to quilt by herself. When her own family needed quilts, she would piece rather easy ones like Trip Around the World, Broken Dishes, and Tumbling Blocks for the family to use. She made us girls each four quilts, and the boys three when they left home. When she was about 65 years old, she started quilting for several different quilt shops like Lone Star for some retirement income. She did this until she was 78 years old. The one evening she told me her right hand just didn't want to do what it is supposed to. She couldn't thread the needle and made bigger stitches. I threaded about 12 needles for her every morning before going to work. By evening she had used them all up. This went on until her eyes got cataracts and she hardly could see well enought to make nice, even stitches and felt embarrased to quilt for someone else, so she just gave up quilting. This was rather depressing to her. She makes light meals and does some cleaning for her pastime now. But she has a good mind yet.   —*Effie Hershberger, Quilter*

As long as I can remember, my Mom quilted, so when my sister and I were old enought, we also helped. After I got married, I decided to start quilting for Land of Canaan in Walnut Creek. I started with wallhangers and crib quilts, then after a while I started doing larger quilts. I do have a 1-year-old boy now, so I am not quilting at this time. Maybe I can again in years to come.   —*Freda Yoder*

At home I helped Mom quilt. I thought I would never do quilting in my own home. After I got married, I had some spare time, so I decided I could do some quilting after all. I started in 1979 for different ladies in different states. Then in 1982 I did my first one for Lone Star Quilt Shop. It was a Lone Star quilt. After the girls were old enough, they helped at times, too. We had two daughters, and they are both married now. I am still quilting as time permits. It is my favorite hobby.   —*Anna Yoder, Quilter*

I started quilting in 1937 when I was still at home. I remember Mother teaching us how to make knots. After I got married I quit quilting until our girls were old enough to help. We began by making quilts for all the family members. Except for the eight months I spent recuperating from carpal tunnel surgery, I've been quilting ever since. It's a nice part-time job for me as a widow.   —*Mrs. Emma Schlabach*

Double Wedding Ring

The beautiful Double Wedding Ring is a favorite among quilt lovers. There are many color combinations. The one shown here is an old-fashioned favorite of ours.

Double Wedding Ring

Wedding Foods

Our family has had three weddings for our three daughters. All the food was cooked by eighteen cooks the day before and the day of the wedding. The recipes in this section feature the foods we served at our daughters' weddings and each one feeds about 400 people.

—*Sara Yoder*

Chicken

290 lb. chicken	1 Tbsp. lemon pepper
2 c. flour	2 Tbsp. seasoned salt
1 c. Bisquick	3 c. Runion
1/2 c. cracker crumbs	

Salt chicken and put in layers on ice the day before. Fry, then put in roaster. Cover with foil, and poke holes in foil with fork. Bake at 350° for 2 hours.

Barbecued Hamburgers

4 lb. crushed soda crackers	3 doz. eggs
1 lb. rolled oats	4 c. minced onion
2 loaves bread, soaked	85 lb. hamburger

Mix soda crackers, oats, bread, eggs, and onion. Divide into four parts. Divide the hamburger into four parts. Combine the egg mixture and hamburger. Shape into patties and barbecue the day before the wedding. Cool. Put four layers of hamburgers in a roaster, pouring barbecue sauce on each layer. Bake at 350° for 2 1/2 hours.

Barbecue Sauce

1 c. ketchup	1 Tbsp. mustard
2 Tbsp. brown sugar	2 Tbsp. Worcestershire sauce

Make 16 batches.

Baked Beans

1 gal. pork and beans, drained	2 c. ketchup
1 (16 oz.) can kidney beans	2 Tbsp. mustard
2 c. brown sugar	

Make 4 batches, 1 batch in each roaster. Add 2 c. pork and bean liquid to each roaster. Bake for 1 hour.

Potluck Potatoes

100 potatoes, peeled, cubed

Sauce:

10 lb. sour cream	1 Tbsp. garlic salt
2 lb. butter	4 cans cream of celery soup
2 Tbsp. Lawry's salt	4 cans cream of chicken soup
3 lb. Velveeta cheese	

Topping:

2 boxes Ritz crackers, crushed   butter

Cook potatoes, then divide into 8 large roasters. Pour sauce over potatoes. Bake for 1¹/₂ hours. Add butter to crushed Ritz crackers to moisten. Bake in a separate pan until crunchy. Fill serving bowls with potatoes and top with cracker crumbs. Delicious!

Mashed Potatoes

6 qt. potatoes	¹/₂ c. butter
1 can evaporated milk	hot milk
4 oz. cream cheese	

Cook potatoes until tender. Mash and add evaporated milk, cream cheese, and butter. Add hot milk until you reach the desired consistency. Make 15 batches.

Wedding Dressing (Stuffing)

6 c. chopped chicken	3 c. diced carrots
5 c. diced celery	6-7 loaves bread, cubed, toasted
5 c. cubed potatoes	1 c. chopped parsley

Broth:

16 eggs, beaten	1 Tbsp. salt
8 c. chicken broth	1 Tbsp. black pepper
8 c. milk	1 Tbsp. seasoned salt
1 Tbsp. lemon pepper	

Combine broth ingredients. Pour over remaining ingredients. Fry until browned. Put into roaster and bake.

Gravy

7 qt. broth	1³/₄ c. clear jel
8 egg yolks	2 Tbsp. chicken flavoring
1³/₄ c. flour	1 Tbsp. salt

Gravy

4 c. chicken broth	2 Tbsp. flour
¹/₂ c. clear jel	2 egg yolks

Mix and bring to a boil. Make 4 batches.

Noodles for 90 People

5 cans College Inn chicken broth	1 Tbsp. salt
4 c. cut up chicken	¹/₂ tsp. black pepper
4 cans cream of chicken soup	12 c. water
1 c. butter, browned	4 lb. Inn Maid noodles
3 Tbsp. chicken base	1 lb. Velveeta cheese

Mix first 8 ingredients together; bring to a boil. Add noodles, then bring to a boil again. Add Velveeta cheese. Stir a little, then let set for 1¹/₂ hours. Makes a 20-quart canner ³/₄ full.

Ham & Potato Soup

6 lb. ham, cubed	pepper
6 qt. potatoes, cubed	seasoned salt
8 c. celery, diced	2 c. butter
2 lg. onions, diced	3 c. flour
8 c. carrots, diced	2¹/₂-3 gal. milk
salt	2 lb. Velveeta cheese

Combine potatoes, celery, onions, carrots, salt, pepper, and seasoned salt. Add a little liquid and cook until vegetables are tender; drain. Heat butter and flour together until some is roasted. Add milk, vegetables, and ham, and heat to almost boiling. Turn off heat and add Velveeta cheese. Keep warm, but don't boil. Yields 24-26 qt.

Potato Salad

12 c. cubed, cooked potatoes	¹/₂ med. onion
12 hard-boiled eggs	1¹/₂ c. chopped celery

Dressing:

3 c. salad dressing	2¹/₂ c. sugar
6 Tbsp. mustard	4 tsp. salt
¹/₄ c. vinegar	¹/₂ c. milk

Mix together. Make 16 batches.

Cole Slaw

1 head cabbage	$^1/_2$ Tbsp. celery seed
1 c. celery	$^1/_2$ c. vinegar
1 green pepper	2 c. sugar
2 tsp. salt	1 tsp. salt

Mix together cabbage, celery, green pepper, and 2 tsp. salt. Add celery seed, vinegar, sugar, and 1 tsp. salt; mix with slaw. Will keep up to 2 weeks in refrigerator. Make 15 batches.

Salad

20 heads lettuce   your favorite salad vegetables

Sweet & Sour Dressing:

1 c. minced onion	$^1/_4$ c. water
1 c. white sugar	2 Tbsp. salad dressing
$^1/_2$ c. oil	1 tsp. salt
$^1/_4$ c. vinegar	1 tsp. celery salt

Make 14 batches dressing.

Relish Dip

2 c. sour cream	$^1/_2$ tsp. dill weed
1$^1/_2$ env. Ranch dressing mix	$^1/_2$ tsp. seasoned salt

Serve with your favorite vegetables.

Dinner Rolls

You will need 28 dozen dinner rolls.

Angel Food Dessert

1 angel food cake   strawberry pie glaze
strawberries, sliced

Filling:

8 oz. cream cheese	2 c. Rich's topping
$^1/_2$ c. powdered sugar	

Cut up angel food cake. Layer with filling, strawberry slices, and glaze. Make 20 batches.

Fruit Dip

14 c. marshmallow crème
11 (8 oz.) pkg. cream cheese
  Serve with your favorite fruit.

3 c. pineapple juice
8 c. powdered sugar

Fruit Glaze

4 c. pineapple juice
1 c. peach juice
  Cook together and simmer for 15 minutes. When cool, add:

$^3/_4$ c. clear jel
1 c. sugar

3 gal. pineapple tidbits
14 qt. peaches
12 c. apples
  Make 9 batches.

7 lb. red grapes
7 lb. green grapes

Strawberry Pie Glaze

1 pkg. strawberry Jell-O
3 c. water and 7-Up
  Make 40 batches.

1 c. sugar
3 Tbsp. clear jel

Date Pudding

2 c. dates, cut up
2 c. boiling water
1 tsp. soda
2 Tbsp. butter
2 c. sugar

2 eggs
2 tsp. vanilla
3 c. flour
$^1/_2$ tsp. salt

Caramel Sauce:
$^1/_2$ c. butter
2 c. brown sugar
3 c. water
$^1/_2$ c. clear jel
2 eggs, beaten

1 Tbsp. flour
$^1/_2$ c. water
salt
vanilla or maple flavoring

  Combine dates, boiling water, soda, and butter. Mix well and let set until cool. Add remaining ingredients and bake at 350° until done. For caramel sauce, heat butter and brown sugar until caramelized. Be careful not to burn it. Add 3 c. water; cook until dissolved. Mix clear jel, eggs, flour, and $^1/_2$ c. water. Add to brown sugar mixture and cook together. Add salt and flavoring. Make 8 batches.

Date Pudding Blocks

1 c. chopped dates	1 egg, beaten
1 c. boiling water	1 tsp. vanilla
1 Tbsp. butter	$^1/_2$ c. nuts
1 tsp. soda	1 c. Thesco flour
1 c. brown sugar	

Sauce:

$^1/_2$ c. butter, melted	1 tsp. vanilla or $^1/_2$ tsp. maple flavoring
3 c. brown sugar	$^3/_4$ c. clear jel
$^1/_4$ tsp. salt	$^1/_2$ c. water

Mrs. Susan Kauffman, Quilter

Ice Cream & Cake

500 squares ice cream	3 chocolate sheet cakes
5 white sheet cakes	

Bake sheet cakes with 2 batches batter per pan.

a Stitch in Time

Select good quality material for a quilt backing to help the quilt wear well.

If we think about the problems women of previous generations encountered while we stitch, our difficulties will fall into a healthy perspective.

Since fabrics are discontinued regularly, always buy extra in case you need more than anticipated later.

When ironed, freezer paper will stick to fabric.

Star in Log Cabin

The star and log cabin designs are all-time favorites. The Star in Log Cabin quilt features both. The center star is the prominent feature if the colors are chosen with care.

Breads & Rolls

Star in Log Cabin

Bread

2¹/₂ c. boiling water	¹/₂ c. oil (scant)
3 c. cold water	¹/₂ c. lard (scant)
2 Tbsp. yeast	1 Tbsp. salt
¹/₂ c. sugar	3 Tbsp. light Karo or honey
¹/₂ c. brown sugar	

Mix hot water and cold water. Dissolve yeast in water, then add sugars. Stir in oil, lard, Karo, and salt. Let rise for 30 minutes; punch down. Let rise another 30 minutes; punch down. Add 3 c. whole wheat flour and enough white flour to reach desired consistency. Yields 8 loaves.

Miss Anna D. Hershberger, Quilt Piecer

Very Good Bread

¹/₃ c. sugar	2 c. cold water
¹/₃ c. brown sugar	2 Tbsp. yeast
1 tsp. salt	³/₄ c. Wesson oil
3 Tbsp. flour	8¹/₄ c. bread flour
1 c. boiling water	

Combine sugars, salt, flour, water, and yeast. Mix together and let rise until bubbly. Add oil and bread flour. Knead down every 15 minutes for 1 hour. Shape into 5 loaves and let rise for 2¹/₂ hours. Bake at 350° for 30 minutes.

Katy Yoder, Quilt Piecer

Simple but Good Bread

¹/₃ c. brown sugar	2 Tbsp. yeast
¹/₃ c. sugar	2 Tbsp. salt
3 Tbsp. flour	6 c. bread flour
1 c. boiling water	³/₄ c. oil
2 c. cold water	

Combine sugars, 3 Tbsp. flour, and boiling water. Stir until sugar is dissolved. Add cold water, then yeast and salt. Let set until yeast begins to work, then add oil. Add 6 c. flour; knead. Let rise, punching down every 15 minutes, for 1 hour. Put into bread pans. Bake at 350° for 35 minutes or until done.

Freda Miller

White Bread

2 Tbsp. yeast	$^3/_4$ c. oil
1 Tbsp. sugar	$^1/_2$ c. sugar
2 c. water	1 c. water
2 c. flour	$6^1/_2$ c. flour
$^3/_4$ Tbsp. salt	

Combine yeast, 1 Tbsp. sugar, and 2 c. water. Let rise slightly. Add 2 c. flour and salt. Let rise 30 minutes. Add oil, $^1/_2$ c. sugar, 1 c. water, and $6^1/_2$ c. flour. Let rise 30 minutes. Punch down and let rise until double. Work out into pans.

Mrs. Nelson E. Weaver, Quilter

Whole Wheat Bread

1 pkg. or 1 Tbsp. yeast	$^1/_4$ c. lard, melted
$^1/_2$ c. warm water	1 c. cool water
1 c. milk, scalded	4 c. white flour
$^1/_2$ c. brown sugar	2 c. whole wheat flour
1 Tbsp. salt	

Soak yeast in warm water. Combine milk, brown sugar, salt, and lard until dissolved. Add yeast mixture and cool water. Add flour. Let rise until double. Put in pans and let rise. Bake.

Sara Yoder

Dinner Rolls

3 c. hot milk	3 eggs
$^1/_2$ c. sugar	2 Tbsp. yeast
1 Tbsp. salt	7 c. flour
5 Tbsp. shortening	

Combine milk, sugar, salt, and shortening; cool. Stir in yeast. Add 2 c. flour. Beat in eggs and add remaining flour. Let rise twice. Bake for 20 minutes. Do not overbake.

Sara Yoder

Dinner Rolls

4 c. milk, scalded	9 eggs, beaten
1³/₄ c. margarine	4 Tbsp. yeast
1³/₄ c. sugar	1 c. warm water
7 tsp. salt (heaping)	18 c. flour

Combine milk and margarine; cool. Combine water and yeast; add to milk. Add salt, sugar, and eggs; mix well. Add flour; knead. Let rise till double. Punch down. Shape into rolls. Let rise. Bake at 350° until done. This recipe can easily be halved or quartered for smaller batches. Yields 8 doz.

Dinner Rolls

3 c. hot milk	2 eggs, beaten
¹/₂ c. margarine	2 pkg. yeast
³/₄ c. sugar	3 c. donut mix
1 Tbsp. salt	6-7 c. flour

Combine milk, margarine, sugar, and salt; cool. Add eggs, yeast, donut mix, and flour. Let rise for 1 hour.

Mrs. Henry A. Hershberger, Quilt Piecer

Yeast Rolls

1 pkg. dry yeast	3 Tbsp. sugar
¹/₄ c. lukewarm water	1¹/₂ tsp. salt
1 tsp. sugar	4 Tbsp. shortening, melted
1 c. scalded milk	3¹/₂ c. bread flour
1 egg, well beaten	

Combine yeast, warm water, and 1 tsp. sugar. Mix with milk, 3 Tbsp. sugar, salt, and shortening, then cool to lukewarm. Add egg to the mixture and as much flour as needed. Let rise 1 hour. Punch down. Let rise until double. Bake at 350°.

Mrs. Dan Schlabach, Quilter

Mile-High Biscuits

3 c. sifted flour	4¹/₂ tsp. baking powder
³/₄ tsp. cream of tartar	2¹/₂ Tbsp. sugar
³/₄ tsp. salt	³/₄ c. shortening
1 egg, lightly beaten	1 c. milk

Mix dry ingredients together. Cut in shortening. Add beaten egg to milk. Add liquid to dry ingredients and mix with fork until dough holds together. Knead lightly. Roll to 1" thick and cut. Use only enough flour to handle dough easily. Bake at 450° for 12 minutes or until brown. Yields 24 biscuits.

Mrs. Joe M. Miller

Whole Wheat Butterhorns

2³/₄ c. flour, divided   ¹/₂ c. butter or margarine, divided
2 pkg. dry yeast   2 Tbsp. honey
1³/₄ c. water, divided   2 tsp. salt
¹/₃ c. brown sugar   2 c. whole wheat flour

Put 1¹/₂ c. flour into a large mixing bowl. Dissolve yeast in ³/₄ c. lukewarm water. Heat 1 c. water, brown sugar, honey, 3 Tbsp. butter, and salt to 120°-130°. Add to flour, then add dissolved yeast. Beat on low speed for 30 seconds; increase speed to high and continue beating for 3 minutes. Stir in whole wheat flour and enough remaining flour to form a soft dough. Turn onto a lightly floured surface and knead until smooth and elastic, 6-8 minutes. Place in a greased bowl, turning once to grease top. Cover and allow to rise until double. Punch dough down and divide into thirds. Shape into a ball; cover and let rest for 10 minutes. Roll each ball into a 12" circle on a floured board. Cut each circle into 8 wedges. Roll wedges into crescent shapes, beginning at wide end. Place on greased cookie sheets. Cover and let rise until double. Melt remaining butter and brush over each roll. Bake at 400° for 10-15 minutes or until golden brown. Brush again with butter while hot.

Mrs. David A. Miller

Sweet French Buns

1 pkg. yeast   3 Tbsp. butter
¹/₄ c. lukewarm water   1 tsp. salt
¹/₂ tsp. sugar   1 large egg, beaten
1 c. milk, scalded   4 c. Robin Hood flour
¹/₄ c. sugar

Combine yeast, water, and ¹/₂ tsp. sugar. Combine milk, ¹/₄ c. sugar, butter, and salt; cool to lukewarm. Add egg to milk mixture. Add yeast; mix well. Stir in flour. Let rise until double; punch down and let rise again. Bake at 325° for 30 minutes or until done. Yields 2 doz.

Mrs. Steven Yoder

Morning Glory Muffins

2 c. flour
1 tsp. soda
2 tsp. cinnamon
1/2 tsp. nutmeg
1 1/4 c. sugar

2 c. grated carrots
2 grated apples
3/4 c. raisins
1 c. oil
3 eggs

Combine flour, soda, cinnamon, nutmeg, and sugar. Add remaining ingredients; mix until moistened. Put into muffin pans and bake at 350° for 20-25 minutes.

Ada Marie Miller, Quilt Piecer

Cinnamon Rolls

1 pkg. yeast
1/4 c. lukewarm water
1 c. milk, scalded
1/3 c. melted butter

1/3 c. sugar
3 eggs, well beaten
1/2 tsp. salt
3 3/4 c. flour

Dissolve yeast in water. Combine sugar, butter, salt, and milk; cool to lukewarm. Add yeast mixture, eggs, and flour to make a stiff batter. Let rise until double. Knead and let rise again. Roll out. Let rise 30 minutes. Bake.

Lizzie Yoder, Quilt Piecer

Cinnamon Rolls

2 c. warm water
1 tsp. salt (scant)
1/2 c. sugar
2 pkg. yeast

1/4 c. Wesson oil
2 eggs, well beaten
6 c. flour

Roll with butter, sugar, and cinnamon. Bake at 325° for 15 minutes or until golden. Yields 2 large cake pans full.

Verna Gingerich, Quilter

Sour Cream Rolls

1 pkg. dry yeast
1/4 c. warm water
1/4 c. sugar
1/2 tsp. salt

1/2 c. sour cream
6 Tbsp. butter
2 eggs, beaten
2 3/4-3 c. flour

Glaze:
³/₄ c. brown sugar   ¹/₄ c. butter, melted
¹/₂ c. sour cream

Soften yeast in warm water. Stir in sugar, salt, sour cream, butter, and eggs. Gradually add flour to make a stiff dough, beating well after each addition. Cover; let rise in warm place until light and doubled, about 2 hours. Knead dough on a well-floured surface 15 times. Roll out half of dough to a 12" circle. Brush with 2 Tbsp. butter. Mix together 1 c. brown sugar and cinnamon. Use half for each half of dough. Sprinkle over dough. Cut into 12 pie-shaped pieces. Roll up, starting with wide end. Put point side down in a 9x13 pan. Repeat with other half of dough and cinnamon/sugar mixture. Make 3 rows of 8 rolls in pan. Cover and let rise. Bake at 350° for 25-30 minutes. Pour glaze over hot rolls. Sprinkle with nuts, if desired.

Clara Yoder, Quilt Marker

Maple Twist Rolls

³/₄ c. milk   1 tsp. maple flavoring
¹/₄ c. butter   ¹/₂ tsp. salt
1 Tbsp. yeast   3 Tbsp. sugar
warm water   3 c. flour
1 egg

Filling:
¹/₄ c. butter   1 tsp. maple flavoring
¹/₂ c. brown sugar   ¹/₃ c. nuts
1 tsp. cinnamon

Glaze:
2 c. powdered sugar   2 tsp. milk
1 Tbsp. butter   ¹/₂ tsp. maple flavoring

Heat milk and butter until warm. Dissolve yeast in warm water. Beat together egg, flavoring, salt, and sugar; add flour. Combine all ingredients. Let rise, then put on a large cookie sheet. Put filling on top. Cut 16 wedges and twist each one. Let rise.

Mrs. James (Linda) Weaver, Quilt Piecer

Apple Rolls

2 Tbsp. sugar	2 c. flour
3 Tbsp. butter or lard	2 tsp. baking powder
1 egg	4 chopped apples
1/2 c. milk	

Syrup:

1 c. sugar	1/2 c. water

Spread dough with butter. Sprinkle with a little cinnamon. Put apples over the dough. Roll up and cut like cinnamon rolls. Pour syrup over rolls; bake. Serve with milk and sugar.

Mrs. Eli D. Yoder

Cream Sticks

1 c. milk, scalded, cooled	3/4 c. sugar
2 pkg. dry yeast	2 eggs, beaten
1 c. lukewarm water	1 tsp. salt
1/2 c. shortening	6 c. flour

Cream Filling:

3 tsp. flour	1 c. sugar
1 c. milk	1 Tbsp. vanilla
1 c. Crisco	2 1/2 c. powdered sugar

Dissolve yeast in warm water. Cream shortening, sugar, eggs, and salt. Add yeast mixture and milk. Add flour to form a soft dough. Let rise in a warm place until double. Roll out and cut into strips. When raised, deep fat fry. Cool. For cream filling, mix flour and milk. Bring to a boil, stirring constantly. Cool completely. Cream together Crisco, sugar, and vanilla. Mix with milk mixture. Add powdered sugar. Fill cream sticks. Make brown sugar icing to cover them.

Mrs. Eli E. Zook, Quilter

Buttermilk Donuts

1 pkg. dry yeast	3/4 c. warm buttermilk
1/4 c. water	1/2 c. mashed potatoes
1/4 c. sugar	1 egg, beaten
1 tsp. salt	1 tsp. nutmeg
1/4 c. shortening	2 1/2 c. flour

Dissolve yeast in water. Mix together all other ingredients. Stir in yeast. Knead for 5 minutes until smooth. Let rise until double. Put on floured board to roll out. Cut out. Let rise for 30 minutes. Fry in hot oil. Drain. Dust with powdered sugar. Yields 2 doz. donuts.

Sara Yoder

Laura's Donuts

1 c. milk
1/4 c. sugar
1 tsp. salt
1/2 c. lard

2 eggs, well beaten
2 pkg. yeast
3 1/2 c. flour

Scald milk, but do not boil. Put sugar, salt, and shortening in a bowl; add milk. Cool, then add eggs and yeast. Add flour. Let rise 1 hour. Work down. Let rise again. Roll out and cut into donuts. Combine powdered sugar and hot water to make a glaze. Glaze donuts.

Laura Troyer, Quilt Piecer

a Stitch in Time

Our saliva contains an enzyme that neutralizes the proteins of our own blood. To remove a bloodstain, moisten a cotton swab in your mouth and rub the blemish.

A silver pencil works well for marking quilting lines on dark material.

To preserve a quilt which requires folding for storage, use generous amounts of acid-free tissue paper in each fold to prevent creases.

Trail of Stars

Long hours of trial and error went into the Trail of Stars pattern. Ada Marie and I worked hard to get every piece to fit together perfectly. Trail of Stars is one of our original designs and the pattern, as well as the finished quilts, are available.

Breakfast

Trail of Stars

Breakfast Pizza

1 lb. bulk sausage	5 eggs
1 pkg. crescent rolls	$1/4$ c. milk
1 c. frozen hash browns	$1/2$ tsp. salt
1 c. shredded cheddar cheese	$1/8$ tsp. pepper
2 Tbsp. Parmesan cheese	

In a skillet, brown sausage. Separate and roll crescent dough into 8 triangles. Place on ungreased 12" pizza pan, points toward center. Press over bottom and up sides to form crusts. Spoon sausage over crust. Sprinkle with potatoes. Top with cheese. In a bowl, beat together eggs, milk, salt, and pepper. Pour into crust. Sprinkle with Parmesan cheese. Bake at 375° for 20-30 minutes.

Rosie Hershberger, Quilt Piecer

Breakfast Pizza

2 pkg. crescent rolls	6 eggs, scrambled, half done
1 lb. sausage	Velveeta cheese
3 c. home fries	2 lb. bacon
1 can cream of mushroom soup	

Bake rolls until half done. Top with sausage, then potatoes. Drizzle mushroom soup over top. Bake until you have eggs ready. Top with eggs, then Velveeta cheese and bacon.

Lydia Yoder, Quilter

Breakfast Casserole

6 eggs, beaten	chopped onion
ham, bacon, or sausage, browned	1 tsp. dry mustard
salt	2 c. milk
pepper	6 pieces bread, cubed

Mix all together and pour into a greased 9x12 pan. Refrigerate overnight. Remove from refrigerator and top with Velveeta cheese slices. Bake at 350° for 30 minutes.

Mattie Miller, Quilter

Ham & Egg Omelet

5 eggs	1 Tbsp. flour (heaping)
pepper to taste	1 c. milk
$1/2$ lb. ham, cubed	1 tsp. baking powder

Mrs. Abe J. Yoder, Quilter

Sausage & Egg Casserole

12 eggs	1 pkg. sausage, browned, drained
4 c. milk	2 tsp. dry mustard
6 slices bread, cubed	salt
3 c. shredded cheese	pepper

Beat the eggs and milk; add to remaining ingredients. Mix. Pour into a baking dish. Cover and set in refrigerator for several hours or overnight. Bake, uncovered, at 350° for 1 hour.

Mrs. Ella Keim, Quilt Piecer

Poor Valley Waffles

2¹/₂ c. flour	2 c. buttermilk or sour milk
1 tsp. salt	1 tsp. soda
¹/₂ c. melted butter or margarine	3 eggs, separated
1 tsp. baking powder	

Sift dry ingredients together. Add beaten egg yolks, buttermilk, and melted butter. Fold in beaten egg whites last. Bake on a hot, lightly greased griddle.

Sevilla Swartzentruber, Quilter

Country Brunch

16 slices bread, cubed	3 c. milk
2¹/₂ c. ham, cubed	¹/₂ c. chopped onion (optional)
16 oz. cheddar cheese	¹/₂ c. chopped pepper (optional)
6 eggs, beaten	3 c. crushed Ritz crackers
1 small bag Tater-Tots	¹/₂ c. melted butter

Grease a 9x13 pan. Layer bread, ham, Tater-Tots, onion, and pepper. Mix eggs and milk; pour over all. Bake at 350° for 30 minutes. Combine cracker crumbs and butter. Top casserole with cheese, then cracker crumbs. Bake 15-30 minutes longer. Let set 15 minutes before serving. Yields 12-15 servings.

Sara Yoder

Granola Cereal

6 c. oatmeal	1 c. coconut
4 c. whole wheat flour	1¹/₂ c. melted butter
2 c. brown sugar	2 tsp. soda

Mix all together and bake at 300° for 1 hour. Stir every 15 minutes.

Mrs. Henry A. Hershberger, Quilt Piecer

Celtic Rose

The Celtic Rose is made by some of our best quilters. Its pretty roses are eloquently framed with braided trim, making a fabulous statement for any bedroom. This quilt is appliquéd.

Meats & Main Dishes

Celtic Rose

Best Meat Loaf

2 lb. ground beef	2 tsp. salt
3/4 c. quick oats	1/4 tsp. pepper
2 eggs, beaten	1 c. tomato juice
1/4 c. chopped onion	

Sauce:

1/2 c. ketchup	2 Tbsp. brown sugar
1 Tbsp. mustard	

Combine ingredients. Pack firmly into a 9x9 pan. Top with sauce. Bake at 350° for 1 hour. Let set for 5 minutes before slicing.

LeAnna Troyer

Tangy Meatballs

2 eggs	2 tsp. salt
2 c. quick oats	1/2 tsp. black pepper
1 can evaporated milk	1/2 tsp. garlic powder
1/4-1/2 c. chopped onion	3 lb. ground beef

Sauce:

2 c. ketchup	1-2 tsp. liquid smoke
1 1/2 c. brown sugar	1/2 tsp. garlic powder
1/4 c. chopped onion	

In a large bowl, beat eggs. Add oats, milk, onion, salt, pepper, and garlic powder. Add the ground beef; mix well. Shape into 1 1/2" balls. Place into two 9x13 baking pans. Bake, uncovered, at 375° for 30 minutes. Remove from the oven; drain. Place meatballs in one pan. Bring sauce ingredients to a boil; pour over meatballs. Return to the oven and bake, uncovered, for 20 minutes or until meatballs are done. Yields 4 doz.

Clara Yoder, Quilt Marker

Barbecued Hamburger Balls

1 1/2 lb. hamburger	1 c. milk
1 c. oatmeal	salt

Sauce:

chopped onion	3 Tbsp. sugar
1 c. ketchup	3 Tbsp. vinegar
1/2 c. water	1 Tbsp. Worcestershire sauce

Combine ingredients; shape into balls. Roll in flour and fry. Mix sauce ingredients and pour over meatballs. Bake at 350° for 1 1/2 hours.

Anna Hershberger, Quilter

Saucy Meatballs

1 lb. hamburger	$^1/_4$ tsp. salt
$^1/_2$ c. dry bread crumbs	$^1/_2$ tsp. Worcestershire sauce
$^1/_4$ c. milk	1 egg
2 Tbsp. finely chopped onion	

Sauce:

1 can cream of chicken soup	$^1/_8$ tsp. ground nutmeg
$^1/_3$ c. milk	$^1/_2$ c. sour cream

Mix ingredients. Shape into $1^1/_2$" balls. Bake on ungreased cookie sheet at 400° until light brown, about 20 minutes. In a casserole, mix cream of chicken soup, milk, and nutmeg. Add meatballs. Bake at 350° for 30 minutes or until done. Stir in sour cream and bake for 10 minutes longer. Yields about 20 meatballs.

Susan Yoder, Quilter

Meatballs

3 lb. hamburger	$^1/_2$ c. chopped onion
1 can evaporated milk	$^1/_2$ tsp. garlic powder
1 c. oatmeal	2 tsp. salt
1 c. cracker crumbs	2 tsp. pepper
2 eggs	2 tsp. chili powder

Sauce:

2 c. ketchup	$^1/_2$ tsp. liquid smoke
1 c. brown sugar	$^1/_4$ tsp. chopped onion

Mix all ingredients; shape into balls. Combine sauce ingredients. Pour over meatballs. Bake at 350° until done.

Mrs. Susan Kauffman, Quilter

Iowa Ham Balls

2 c. graham cracker crumbs	2 lb. ground beef
2 lb. turkey ham, finely chopped	$1^1/_2$ c. milk

Sauce:

2 cans condensed tomato soup	$1^1/_2$ c. brown sugar
2 tsp. dry mustard	$^1/_4$ c. vinegar

Mix ingredients; shape into balls. Combine sauce ingredients and pour over ham balls. Bake, uncovered, at 350° for 1 hour.

Katy Yoder, Quilt Piecer

Stuffed Burgers

2 lb. ground beef
1 c. shredded cheese
1/3 c. chopped green pepper
1/3 c. chopped tomatoes
3 fresh mushrooms, chopped

2 green onions, chopped
1/2 c. barbecue sauce
1 Tbsp. sugar
4 hamburger buns

Shape beef into 8 patties. In a bowl, combine cheese, peppers, tomatoes, mushrooms, and onions. Top half of the patties with vegetable mixture. Cover with remaining patties and firmly press edges to seal. Grill or broil for 3 minutes on each side. Brush with barbecue sauce and sprinkle with sugar. Grill or broil 10-15 minutes longer or until no longer pink.

Ina Yoder

Mini Crescent Burgers

1 lb. ground beef
1 c. shredded cheddar cheese

1 env. onion soup mix
3 (8 oz.) tubes crescent rolls

In a skillet, cook beef over medium heat until no longer pink; drain. Stir in cheese and soup mix; set aside. Separate crescent dough into triangles; cut each one in half lengthwise, forming two triangles. Place 1 Tbsp. beef mixture along the wide end of each triangle. Roll up. Place, pointed side down, 2" apart on ungreased baking sheets. Bake at 375° for 15 minutes.

Ina Yoder

Oven-Barbecued Pork Chops

6-8 pork chops

Sauce:
1 Tbsp. Worcestershire sauce
2 Tbsp. vinegar
2 tsp. brown sugar
1/2 tsp. pepper

1/2 tsp. chili powder
1/2 tsp. paprika
3/4 c. ketchup
1/3 c. hot water

Put pork chops in bottom of a 9x13 pan. Pour sauce on top. Bake at 375° for 1 hour.

Rosie Hershberger, Quilt Piecer

Charcoal Broiled Steak

1/2 c. salad oil   1/8 tsp. black pepper
2 Tbsp. lemon juice   1/2 tsp. season all
1/8 tsp. garlic powder   1 tsp. Worcestershire sauce
1 tsp. onion salt   3-4 lb. 1" thick steaks

Mix together first 7 ingredients. Marinate steak in mixture for several hours. Cook over hot charcoal for 3 minutes on each side.

Laura Yoder, Quilter

Fried Chicken

2 c. flour   3 Tbsp. seasoned salt
2 c. finely crushed crackers   1 1/2 tsp. black pepper
1/2 Tbsp. paprika   6 tsp. Ac'cent
1 Tbsp. sugar   2 1/2 tsp. garlic salt

Salt chicken lightly the day before. Combine the above ingredients and roll chicken in mixture. Fry chicken. Pour 1/2 cup water into roaster, then line with foil. Put chicken into roaster, then cover with foil. Cut several slits into foil. Bake at 350° for 1 1/2 hours. For weddings, make 6 batches of this mixture for 200 lb. chicken.

Mrs. Ella Keim, Quilt Piecer

Chicken Nuggets

Batter:
2 eggs   1 c. self-rising flour
2/3 c. milk   2 Tbsp. oil

Crumbs:
2 pkg. soda crackers, crushed   1 1/2 tsp. pepper
2 1/2 tsp. salt   1 tsp. paprika

Barbecue Sauce:
1/3 c. ketchup   1 tsp. mustard
2 Tbsp. brown sugar

Dip chicken chunks into batter, then roll in crumbs. Deep fry in canola oil at 350° until done. Serve with barbecue sauce for dipping.

Mrs. Junior Weaver, Quilt Marker

Chicken Bites

4 chicken breasts
1 c. Ritz cracker crumbs
1/2 c. Parmesan cheese
1/4 c. finely grated walnuts
1 tsp. basil

1 tsp. thyme
1/2 tsp. seasoning salt
1/4 tsp. pepper
1/2 c. melted butter

Cut chicken into bite-sized pieces. Combine dry ingredients to make a crumb mixture. Dip chicken into melted butter, then into crumbs. Place chicken 1/2" apart on foil-lined baking sheets. Bake at 400° for 20-25 minutes or until done. Good dipped in ketchup. Yields 4-6 servings.

Lucinda Yoder, Quilt Appliqués

French-fried Chicken

2 eggs
1/2 c. milk
1 tsp. baking powder

1 c. flour
1 tsp. salt
saltines and corn flakes, crushed

Combine eggs and milk; beat. Combine remaining ingredients. Dip chicken into first mixture, then roll in second mixture.

Mrs. Mary N. Zook, Quilter

Chicken Coating Mix

Coating Mix:
1 c. Bisquick
1/2 c. cracker crumbs
1 Tbsp. lemon pepper

2 Tbsp. Lawry's salt
1 Tbsp. salt
4 c. Runion's coating mix

Batter:
1 egg, beaten

1/2-1 c. milk

Dip chicken in batter, then roll in coating mix. Fry and bake until done.

Amanda Yoder, Quilter

Chicken Supreme

2 c. cooked, diced chicken
2 c. uncooked macaroni
2 cans cream of chicken or
　cream of mushroom soup
2 c. milk

1/2 c. chopped onion
1/2 tsp. salt
1/4 tsp. pepper
3 Tbsp. butter
1 c. Velveeta cheese

Combine all ingredients; put in greased casserole. Refrigerate over-night. Bake at 350° for 1½ hours.

Variation: Cook macaroni until almost tender. Add remaining ingredients except milk. Bake at 350° for 30 minutes.

Freida Yoder, Quilter

Chicken Gravy

4½ c. chicken broth	2 Tbsp. flour
1½ Tbsp. chicken soup base	1 egg yolk
⅛ tsp. garlic salt	½ c. milk
5 Tbsp. clear jel	

Combine broth, soup base, and garlic salt. Bring to a boil. Remove from heat. Mix clear jel and flour; add a little milk and stir. Add egg yolk and remaining milk. Gradually stir into hot broth. Return to low heat and continue stirring until thickened. Yields 5 cups.

LeAnna Troyer

Hobos

1 head cabbage, cut fine	sliced onion
sliced potatoes	hamburger patties
sliced carrots	

Put a hamburger pattie and individual portions of remaining ingredients on squares of heavy-duty foil, shiny side up. Use 2 pieces of foil. Fold and lightly seal ingredients inside. Put on rack over hot coals for 15 minutes on each side. When done, open up and add butter and salt.

Sara Yoder

Cheeseburger Quickie

9" baked pie shell	3 eggs, beaten
½ lb. ground beef	1½ c. grated or cubed cheese
⅓ c. onion	½ tsp. salt
½ c. salad dressing	⅛ tsp. pepper
½ c. milk	¼ tsp. oregano

Fry ground beef and onion together. Combine salad dressing, milk, and eggs; beat together. Add cheese, salt, pepper, and oregano. Add to meat and put into baked pie shell. Bake at 350° for 30-35 minutes.

Mrs. Emma Schlabach, Quilter

Shipwreck Casserole

1½ lb. hamburger
onion
salt
4 c. cubed potatoes
2 c. carrots
2 c. peas
diced celery
1 can cream of chicken soup
1 can cream of mushroom soup
milk
Velveeta cheese

Brown hamburger with onion and salt. Add salt to each vegetable. Cook each vegetable until soft. Add celery. Layer hamburger and vegetables in a casserole. Add soups; add milk to reach desired consistency. Bake at 350° until heated through. Top with Velveeta cheese. This is good as a one-dish meal. Serve with applesauce and fruit.

Mrs. Christ Miller

Yumasetta

2 lb. hamburger
salt
pepper
brown sugar
¼ c. chopped onion
1 can tomato soup
1 can cream of chicken soup
1 (16 oz.) pkg. noodles
1 (8 oz.) pkg. processed cheese

Brown hamburger with salt, pepper, brown sugar, and onion. Add tomato soup. Cook noodles; drain. Add cream of chicken soup. Layer hamburger mixture and noodle mixture in casserole with cheese between layers. Bake at 350° for 30 minutes.

Ada, Quilter

Quick & Easy Rice Casserole

1 lb. hamburger
onion
1 can cream of mushroom soup
1 can cream of chicken soup
½ c. uncooked rice
2 c. water

Mix all together and add salt and pepper to taste. Turn into a buttered casserole. Bake at 350° for 1 hour.

Mrs. Emma Schlabach, Quilter

Wigglers

1½ lb. hamburger
5 slices bacon
2 small onions
1 can cream of mushroom soup
1 c. peas
4 c. tomato soup

1½ c. diced potatoes
1½ c. diced carrots
1½ c. diced celery

2 lb. Velveeta cheese
1 lb. spaghetti, cooked

Cook vegetables separately. Fry bacon; remove from skillet. Fry hamburger and onions in bacon drippings. Put into a roaster. Add potatoes, celery, carrots, and peas. Add cream of mushroom soup and spaghetti. Arrange bacon on top. Add grated cheese. Pour tomato soup on top. Bake at 350° for 1-1½ hours.

Mrs. Eli E. Zook, Quilter

Wiggles

3 lb. hamburger
5 slices bacon
3 onions
3 c. diced potatoes
3 c. sliced celery
3 c. diced carrots

2 cans cream of mushroom soup
1 pkg. spaghetti, cooked
2 cans peas
6-8 c. tomato soup
1 lb. cheese

Fry bacon; remove from skillet. Fry hamburger and onions in bacon grease. Put in roaster. Add cooked potatoes, carrots, peas, and raw celery. Add mushroom soup and spaghetti. Arrange bacon slices on top. Add grated cheese. Pour tomato soup over top and bake for 1 hour or until done. Add salt to vegetables to taste, and add a little sugar to tomato soup.

Lizzie Yoder, Quilt Piecer

Lasagna

2 lb. hamburger
2½ c. pizza sauce
2¼ c. tomato juice
¼ tsp. garlic salt
1 tsp. salt
1 tsp. pepper

¼ tsp. oregano
8 oz. lasagna noodles
2 Tbsp. salad oil
1 lb. Velveeta cheese
Parmesan or mozzarella cheese

Fry hamburger until brown. Add spices, pizza sauce, and juice. Cover and simmer for 20 minutes. Don't make the meat sauce too thin. Cook noodles in salt water and the oil. In a casserole, layer meat mixture, noodles, and cheese until everything is used up. Bake at 325° for 20 minutes.

Fannie Troyer, Quilt Binder

Spaghetti Pie

1 (7 oz.) pkg. spaghetti
1 Tbsp. butter
$^1/_3$ c. Parmesan cheese
2 eggs, well beaten
1 c. cottage cheese

1 lb. ground beef
$^1/_2$ c. chopped onion
$^1/_4$ c. chopped green pepper
1 (15$^1/_2$ oz.) jar spaghetti sauce
$^1/_2$ c. shredded mozzarella cheese

Cook spaghetti according to directions on package. Add butter, cheese, and eggs to hot spaghetti. Form mixture into crust in a 10" pie plate. Spread cottage cheese over spaghetti crust. Set aside. Brown hamburger, onions, and peppers. Stir in spaghetti sauce. Put mixture on crust. Bake at 350° for 20 minutes. Sprinkle cheese on top. Return to oven for 5 minutes. Yields 6 servings.

Marlene Yoder

Haystack

3 pkg. bacon crackers
1 lb. rice, cooked
2 sm. heads lettuce, cut up
12 med. tomatoes, cut up
16 hard-boiled eggs, chopped
Velveeta cheese

2 pkg. Doritos
4$^1/_2$ lb. hamburger, browned
1 lg. can Ragù sauce
4 cans cheddar cheese soup
2 soup cans milk

Add Ragù sauce to meat. Mix cheddar cheese soup with milk. Serve ingredients in order listed. Yields 12 servings.

Mrs. Mose Keim, Quilter

Party Beef Casserole

3 Tbsp. flour
1 tsp. salt
$^1/_2$ tsp. pepper
2 lb. boneless round steak,
    cut into $^1/_2$" cubes
2 Tbsp. cooking oil
1 c. water
$^1/_2$ c. beef broth

1 garlic clove, minced
1 Tbsp. dried onion
2 c. fresh or canned mushrooms
2 c. frozen peas
3 c. mashed potatoes
1 Tbsp. butter, melted
paprika

In a large resealable plastic bag, combine flour, salt, and pepper. Add beef cubes; shake to coat. Brown beef in oil over medium heat. Place beef and drippings in a greased, shallow 2$^1/_2$-quart baking dish. Add water, broth, garlic, and onion to skillet. Bring to a boil and simmer, uncovered, for 5 minutes. Stir in mushrooms. Add to meat; mix well.

Bake, covered, at 350° for 1¹/₂-1³/₄ hours or until beef is tender. Sprinkle peas over meat. Spread potatoes on top. Brush with butter; sprinkle with paprika. Bake 15-20 minutes longer.

Ina Yoder

Pizza Casserole

1 lb. hamburger   1 stick sliced pepperoni
onion   2 jars pizza sauce
¹/₂ pkg. noodles, cooked, drained   2 lg. pkg. shredded pizza cheese

Brown hamburger and onion; drain. Cover bottom of 9x13 pan with 1 jar pizza sauce. Add noodles. Sprinkle hamburger over noodles. Add the remaining sauce. Top with cheese and pepperoni. Bake, covered, at 325° for 45 minutes. Uncover and bake 15 minutes longer.

Miss Lizzie E. Zook, Quilter

Pizza Casserole

1¹/₃ c. flour   1 sm. onion, diced
2 tsp. baking powder   ¹/₂ c. spaghetti, cooked, drained
²/₃ tsp. salt   2 c. pizza sauce
¹/₂ c. milk   1 c. sour cream
¹/₄ c. oil   3 c. grated cheese
2¹/₂ lb. hamburger

Mix flour, baking powder, salt, milk, and oil. Press into a 9x13 pan. Fry hamburger and onion together. Layer hamburger, spaghetti, and pizza sauce on the unbaked crust. Mix sour cream and grated cheese. Spread over top. Bake at 350° for about 1 hour.

German Pizza

1 lb. hamburger   2 Tbsp. butter
¹/₄ c. diced onion   6 med. potatoes, peeled, shredded
¹/₂ c. chopped peppers   3 eggs, beaten
1 tsp. salt   ¹/₃ c. milk
¹/₂ tsp. pepper   2 c. cheddar cheese

Brown beef over medium heat with onion, green pepper, salt, and pepper; drain. Spread potatoes in pan. Top with beef mixture. Combine milk and eggs; pour over meat. Bake, covered, until tender, about 30 minutes. Top with cheese. Let set for 15 minutes. Yields 4-6 servings.

Sara Yoder

Slow Cooker Enchiladas

1 lb. ground beef	$^1/_3$ c. water
1 c. chopped onion	1 tsp. chili powder
$^1/_2$ c. chopped green pepper	$^1/_2$ tsp. salt
1 (16 oz.) can pinto or kidney	$^1/_4$ tsp. pepper
beans, drained, rinsed	1 c. shredded sharp cheddar cheese
1 (10 oz.) can green chilies	6 (6"-7") flour tortillas

In a skillet, cook beef, onion, and green pepper until beef is browned and vegetables are tender; drain. Add the next six ingredients; bring to a boil. Reduce heat; cover and simmer for 10 minutes. In a 5-quart slow cooker, layer about $^3/_4$ c. beef mixture, one tortilla, and about $^1/_3$ c. cheese. Repeat layers. Cover and cook on low for 5-7 hours or until heated through. Yields 4 servings.

Mrs. Floyd Yoder, Quilt Piecer

Mexican Bean Casserole

1 lb. hamburger	shredded lettuce
1 onion	diced tomatoes
1 pkg. taco seasoning	sour cream
$^1/_2$ c. water	taco chips
1 can refried beans	salsa or taco sauce
8 oz. shredded cheddar cheese	

Brown hamburger and onion; add taco seasoning, water, and beans. Place in a casserole and top with cheese. Bake at 350° for 45 minutes. Serve, and top with remaining ingredients.

Sadie Yoder, Quilt Binder

Underground Ham Casserole

4 Tbsp. butter	bacon
$^1/_2$ c. chopped onion	1 c. sour cream
4 c. ham	2 cans cream of mushroom soup
1 tsp. Worcestershire sauce	$1^1/_2$ c. milk
2 c. Velveeta cheese	4 qt. mashed potatoes

Sauté onion and ham in butter. Add Worcestershire sauce, cheese, cream of mushroom soup, and milk until cheese melts. Stir until fairly smooth. Put ham mixture in bottom of roaster. Mash the potatoes until smooth; add sour cream. Spread them over ham and cheese mixture. Sprinkle crumbled bacon on top. Bake at 250° until heated through.

Mrs. Mose Keim, Quilter

Underground Ham Casserole

4 Tbsp. butter	2 cans cream of mushroom soup
1/2 c. chopped onion	1 1/2 c. milk
1 Tbsp. Worcestershire sauce	4 qt. mashed potatoes
4 c. ham	2 c. sour cream
2 c. Velveeta cheese	bacon

Fry onions, Worcestershire sauce, and ham in butter. Put in bottom of roaster. Combine cheese, soup, and milk. Layer over ham. Combine mashed potatoes and sour cream. Spread on top. Top with bacon. Bake at 350° for 1 1/2 hours. Do not add salt.

Mattie Troyer, Quilter

Impossible Swiss Ham Pie

2 c. cubed ham, cooked	3/4 c. Bisquick
1 1/2 c. grated Swiss cheese	3 eggs
1/2 c. chopped onion	1 1/2 c. milk

Put ham, cheese, and onion in a greased baking dish. Beat milk, eggs, and Bisquick until smooth. Pour over other ingredients. Bake at 375° for 30-40 minutes or until a knife inserted in center comes out clean. A delicious breakfast or brunch dish.

Mrs. David A. Miller

Scalloped Potatoes

10 lb. potatoes	1 1/4 c. butter
8 c. milk	1 lb. Velveeta cheese
1 1/3 c. flour	2 tsp. Worcestershire sauce
2 Tbsp. salt	5 lb. ham, cubed
1/2 tsp. pepper	1 med. onion, chopped

Cook potatoes in jackets; cool. Peel potatoes and slice into a large baking dish. Melt butter in saucepan; add flour. Stir well, and add milk, cheese, salt, pepper, and Worcestershire sauce. Heat until cheese is melted. Mix ham and onions with potatoes. Pour cheese mixture over potatoes. Bake at 350° for 1 hour. Yields 25-30 servings.

Susan Miller

Potluck Potatoes

2 lb. potatoes	¹/₄ tsp. pepper
¹/₂ c. butter	2 c. sour cream
1 can cream of mushroom soup	2 c. Velveeta cheese
1 tsp. onion salt	1 tsp. Lawry's salt

Topping:

2 c. crushed corn flakes	¹/₂ c. butter, melted

Slice potatoes. Cook until almost tender. Combine remaining ingredients and heat until cheese is melted. Stir sauce and potatoes together in casserole and cover with corn flakes. Bake at 350° for 45 minutes.

Sarah Troyer, Quilt Piecer
Nettie Yoder, Quilt Piecer

Zesty Herb-Roasted Potatoes

¹/₂ c. Miracle Whip	1 tsp. onion powder
1 tsp. oregano	1 tsp. seasoned salt
1 tsp. garlic powder	5 med. potatoes, quartered

Mix salad dressing, seasoning, and water in a large bowl. Add potatoes; toss to coat. Place potatoes on greased cookie sheet. Bake at 400° for 40 minutes.

Ina Yoder

Potato & Egg Dish

3 lg. potatoes, cooked, sliced	salt
3 hard-boiled eggs	pepper

White Sauce:

3 Tbsp. butter	¹/₂ tsp. salt
2 sm. onions, chopped	3 c. milk
2 Tbsp. flour	

Layer potatoes and eggs in a baking dish. Add salt and pepper to taste. Sauté onions in butter; remove onions. Add flour and salt to butter. Stir until light brown. Add milk and let come to a boil. Add onions. Pour over potatoes and eggs in baking dish. Cover with bread crumbs. Bake until brown on top.

Variation: Use macaroni instead of potatoes.

Mrs. Eli D. Yoder, Quilt Piecer

Lunchbox "Handwiches"

1 loaf frozen bread dough, thawed   1 c. shredded Swiss cheese
2^1/$_2$ c. finely chopped   1 egg yolk
   fully cooked ham   1 Tbsp. water

Allow dough to rise according to package directions. Punch down; divide into 10 equal pieces. Roll each piece into a 5" circle. Place about ^{1}/$_4$ c. ham and 2 Tbsp. cheese on each circle; press filling to flatten. Beat egg yolk and water; brush on edges of circles. Fold into semicircles and pinch edges to seal. Brush tops with egg yolk mixture. Place on greased baking sheet. Bake at 375° for 15-20 minutes, or until golden brown. Serve warm or cold. If desired, cool and freeze. Yields 10 sandwiches.

Mrs. Floyd Yoder, Quilt Piecer

A Warm Sandwich

1 med. onion   2 Tbsp. sugar
1 lb. bologna ^{1}/$_2$-^{3}/$_4$ c. salad dressing
^{1}/$_4$ lb. Velveeta cheese

Grind the onion, bologna, and Velveeta cheese. Add sugar and enough salad dressing to moisten the mixture. A little top milk may also be added. Wrap sandwiches in foil and bake at 300°.

Lucinda Yoder, Quilt Appliqués

Sandwich Spread

1 stalk celery   water
6 red peppers   4 c. vinegar
6 green peppers   5 c. sugar
6 onions   2 c. prepared mustard
6 large cucumbers   1 Tbsp. turmeric
6 green tomatoes   1 c. flour
^{1}/$_2$ c. salt

Grind celery, peppers, onions, cucumbers, and tomatoes. Add salt and some water. Let set for 2 hours. Drain. Add vinegar; cook for 20 minutes. Add remaining ingredients. Cook well, stirring constantly. Put into jars; seal.

Mrs. Alvin S. Miller, Quilt Marker

Homemade Bologna

25 lb. fresh hamburger
³/₄ lb. Tender Quick
³/₄ oz. black pepper
¹/₂ c. sugar
³/₄ Tbsp. garlic powder
5 Tbsp. liquid smoke
6 c. water

Mix hamburger and Tender Quick. Let set overnight. The next morning, add remaining ingredients. Mix well. Press into jars. Process in boiling-water bath for 2 hours.

Mrs. Ella Keim, Quilt Piecer

Mom's Pan Haas

2 qt. liverwurst
6 c. broth or water
2 c. oatmeal
6 Tbsp. graham flour
4 Tbsp. white flour
³/₄ c. cornmeal

Cook slowly for at least 30 minutes. Pour into a cake pan. Refrigerate. Cut into slices and fry in butter.

Sara Yoder

Baked Beans

¹/₂ lb. bacon, cut up
2 sm. onions, chopped
1 c. brown sugar
1 c. ketchup
1 Tbsp. prepared mustard
1 sm. can kidney beans
1 sm. can lima beans
1 med. can pork and beans

Fry bacon until crisp. Sauté onions. Add sugar, ketchup, and mustard. Drain beans and add. Add bacon. Bake at 350° for 1 hour.

Variation: Use hamburger instead of bacon.

Sara Yoder

Spaghetti Sauce

6-10 lb. hamburger
1¹/₂ Tbsp. pepper
3 Tbsp. garlic salt
6 Tbsp. parsley flakes
6 Tbsp. butter
3 (12 oz.) cans tomato sauce
3 cans water
6 qt. tomato juice
3 Tbsp. salt
2 c. sugar
3 onions, chopped
3 peppers, chopped
3 sm. cans mushrooms, chopped
¹/₂ c. cooking oil
2 jars Ragù spaghetti sauce or
   your favorite spaghetti sauce

Brown hamburger with pepper, garlic salt, parsley flakes, and butter. Add remaining ingredients. Cook for 1 hour. Put into jars and process in boiling-water bath for 2 hours. Yields 13 qt.

Mrs. David A. Miller

Spaghetti Sauce

10 qt. tomato juice
2 hot peppers, diced
2 green peppers, diced
10-12 onions
1 clove garlic, crushed

3 stalks celery, diced
5 Tbsp. salt
2$^{1}/_{2}$ c. brown sugar
2 pkg. Mrs. Wages mix
clear jel to thicken

Cook all ingredients together for 2 hours. Put into jars and process in boiling-water bath for 30 minutes.

Ada Marie Miller, Quilt Piecer

Onion Ring Batter

1 c. Bisquick
2 eggs
1 c. evaporated milk

$^{1}/_{4}$ tsp. salt
$^{1}/_{8}$ tsp. cinnamon

Mix together. Slice large onions and dip slices into batter. Deep fry. Delicious!

Ada Marie Miller, Quilt Piecer

a Stitch in Time

Arrange choices of fabric together and then stand at a distance from them to judge how well they blend together.

Weaver Fever

Weaver Fever draws its unique design from the art of basket making. My daughters all loved to piece this one even though it has lots of small pieces. Weaver Fever pattern is available through Lone Star.

Soups

Weaver Fever

Hearty Ham Soup

6 lb. ham chunks	pepper
6 qt. cubed potatoes	seasoned salt
2 qt. celery	2^1/$_2$-3 gal. milk
2 lg. onions	2 c. butter
2 qt. carrots	3 c. flour
salt	2 lb. Velveeta cheese

Cook potatoes, celery, onions, and carrots until tender; drain. Add ham, salt, pepper, and seasoned salt. Melt butter. Add flour; stir over heat until browned. Add 1 gallon milk. Heat until almost boiling. Add ham, vegetables, and remaining milk. Heat through, then add cheese. Do not boil. Yields 24 qt.

Sara Yoder

Hearty Ham Soup

4 c. carrots, diced	1 c. butter or margarine
3 c. potatoes, cubed	1 gal. milk
3 c. onions, diced	6 c. chopped ham or turkey ham
1 c. celery, diced	clear jel
^{1}/$_3$ c. chicken base	2 lb. Velveeta cheese

Cook carrots, potatoes, onions, and celery with chicken base, butter, and water until tender. Add milk and ham. Heat to boiling; thicken with clear jel. Remove from heat; add Velveeta cheese. Yields 2 gal.

Mrs. Abe Byler, Quilter

Chunky Beef Soup

2^1/$_2$ gal. water	4 qt. diced carrots
1^1/$_4$ c. beef soup mix	4 qt. diced potatoes
2 lg. cans College Inn beef broth	3 qt. peas
4 qt. tomato juice	8 c. flour
1 c. sugar	water
1 c. brown sugar	5 lb. hamburger
^{1}/$_4$ c. salt	salt
^{1}/$_2$ c. butter	pepper
2 lg. onions, finely chopped	butter

Cook carrots, potatoes, and peas separately. Add salt. Combine water, soup mix, broth, tomato juice, sugars, salt, butter, and onions. Heat to boiling, then add vegetables. Combine flour and enough water to make a paste to thicken soup. Brown hamburger, salt, and pepper in butter. Add to soup. Process in boiling-water bath for 2 hours. Yields about 21 qt.

Variation: We use more meat and not as much flour.

Mrs. Steven Yoder

Swiss Broccoli Chowder

2 Tbsp. butter
1/2 c. chopped green pepper
1/2 c. chopped onion
1 1/2 Tbsp. flour
1/4 tsp. salt

1 1/2 c. milk
1 1/2 c. chicken broth
1 (9 oz.) pkg. chopped broccoli
1 c. shredded Swiss cheese

In a medium saucepan, melt butter. Add green pepper and onion; cook and stir occasionally until vegetables are crisp-tender, about 6 minutes. Stir in flour and salt. Cook and stir for 1 minute. Stir in milk, broth, and broccoli. Cook and stir occasionally until mixture is smooth and thickened, about 5 minutes. Stir in cheese. Cook and stir until cheese melts and mixture is hot, about 2 minutes.

Fannie Troyer, Quilt Binder

Potato Broccoli Soup

1/2 c. chopped onion
2 Tbsp. butter
2 c. water
2 c. finely diced potatoes

2 c. diced broccoli
2 c. milk
1 c. Velveeta cheese

Cook onion in butter until soft. Add water, salt, potatoes, and broccoli; cook until tender. Add milk; heat. Add flour; boil. Add cheese. Do not boil. Stir.

Sara Yoder

Chili Soup

14 lb. hamburger, browned
kidney beans
2 cans chili beans
6 onions
3 c. flour

6 c. brown sugar
2 Tbsp. salt
2 pkg. chili seasoning
tomato juice

Combine ingredients, adding enough tomato juice to fill a stainless steel canner.

Freda Miller

Taco Soup

2 lb. hamburger	1 can kidney beans
onions	2 c. corn
2 pkg. taco seasoning	salsa
4 c. tomato juice	

Fry hamburger and onion together. Mix together all ingredients except salsa and simmer for 1-2 hours. Add salsa. Serve in the following order: corn chips, soup, cheddar cheese, lettuce, and sour cream.

Marlene Yoder

Old-Fashioned Bean Soup

2 Tbsp. butter	1 tsp. salt
1 c. cooked navy beans	bread cubes
4 c. milk	

Brown butter in a 3-quart saucepan. Add beans; cook for several minutes. Add milk; bring to a boil. Add salt and enough bread to use up most of the milk. Cover and let set for 15 minutes. Stir only slightly with a dipper to bring up beans from the bottom of pan. Good with Swiss cheese and pepper.

Mrs. Effie Hershberger, Quilter

a Stitch in Time

To remove the lines made with a water soluble pencil, spray with a mist bottle filled with cold water.

When the quilting process seems long, think about something pleasant to make the time pass faster. Try contemplating about the character of God.

Families are like quilts, you know;

Stitched in *love* with needles of cure.

Lives *different colors,*

but fitted and joined

By *threads* of memories they share.

Bright patches

of happiness, smiles, and fun;

Some *dark* for the hurts and the tears,

But the *pattern* each *family*

makes for itself

Is *cherished* by *all* through the years.

ABOUT THE QUILT
Ohio Rose

This pattern has been a favorite for many people and it's an easy one to make. It's a blend of yesterday's quilt patterns, but also a good one for a beginner to try. The quilt resembles the state of Ohio.

Pizza Cups

1 lb. hot or mild pork sausage
1 (14 oz.) jar pizza sauce
2 Tbsp. ketchup
1/4 tsp. garlic powder

2 (10 oz.) cans biscuits
shredded mozzarella cheese
grated Parmesan cheese

In a skillet, cook sausage over medium heat; drain. Stir in pizza sauce, ketchup, and garlic powder; set aside. Press biscuits into 20 well-greased muffin cups. Spoon 1-2 Tbsp. of the meat sauce into each biscuit. Top with cheese. Bake at 350° for 10-15 minutes or until golden brown.

Iva, Quilter

Taco Pizza

1 lb. ground beef
2 c. pizza sauce or
    2 (8 oz.) cans tomato sauce
1 pkg. taco seasoning
1/2 lb. Velveeta cheese

8 oz. crescent rolls
1 c. shredded lettuce
1/2 c. chopped tomatoes
sour cream

Brown hamburger; add sauce and seasoning. Bake crescent rolls; prick with fork. Top with hamburger, cheese, lettuce, tomatoes, and sour cream.

Mrs. Floyd Yoder, Quilt Piecer

Vegetable Pizza

Crust:
2 cans crescent rolls or a Bisquick crust

Cream Cheese Layer:
3/4 c. Miracle Whip
1 pkg. Hidden Valley Ranch mix

2 (8 oz.) pkg. cream cheese

Toppings:
3/4 c. cauliflower
3/4 c. carrots
3/4 c. broccoli

3/4 c. onion
1 c. cheese

Spread crescent rolls on cookie sheet, pinching together perforations to seal. Bake for 4 minutes; cool. Cream together cream cheese and Miracle Whip. Add Ranch dressing mix. Spread over crust. Sprinkle with shredded vegetables and cheese. Refrigerate for several hours.

Laura Yoder, Quilter

Apple Pizza

1 1/2 c. flour	1/4 c. butter
1 Tbsp. yeast	1 egg
3 Tbsp. sugar	8 oz. cream cheese
1 tsp. salt	4 Tbsp. sugar
1/2 c. water	apple pie filling
1/4 c. milk	

Combine flour, yeast, 3 Tbsp. sugar, and salt in a large bowl. Heat water, milk, and butter to 120°; add to flour. Add egg. Stir in more flour to make a soft dough. Cover and let rise for 30 minutes. Roll out on a 12" pizza pan. Cover with cream cheese and 4 Tbsp. sugar. Put filling on top. Bake at 350° until edge is golden brown.

Mrs. Joe M. Miller

Fruit Pizza

1/2 c. butter	1 tsp. baking powder
1/2 c. brown sugar	pinch salt
1 egg	1 1/3 c. flour

Cream Cheese Layer:

8 oz. cream cheese	1/2 tsp. vanilla
1/2 c. powdered sugar	1 Tbsp. milk

Glaze:

2 c. pineapple juice	1 Tbsp. clear jel (heaping)
1/2 c. sugar	1-2 Tbsp. Jell-O

For crust, cream together butter, sugar, and egg. Add flour, baking powder, and salt. Press into a greased pizza pan. Bake at 375° for 10 minutes or until light brown. Cream together cream cheese layer ingredients; spread over crust. Top with your favorite fruit, such as apples, peaches, pineapple, grapes, oranges, bananas, and strawberries. Cook glaze until clear. Cool. Spread over fruit.

Sarah Troyer, Quilt Piecer

Fruit Pizza

Crust:

1/2 c. margarine	1 1/3 c. + 1 Tbsp. flour
3/4 c. sugar	1 tsp. baking powder
1 egg	1/4 tsp. salt

Cream Cheese Layer:

8 oz. cream cheese

$^1/_2$ c. sugar

$^1/_2$ tsp. vanilla

2 tsp. pineapple juice

1 c. Cool Whip

Cream together margarine, sugar, and egg. Add flour, baking powder, and salt. Bake at 375° for 10-12 minutes. Do not overbake. Combine cream cheese, sugar, vanilla, and pineapple juice; beat well. Fold in Cool Whip. Spread over cooled crust. Top with your favorite fruit and fruit glaze.

Sara Yoder

Pizza Sauce

$^1/_2$ bushel ripe tomatoes

3 cloves garlic

3 lb. onions

4 hot peppers

2 c. cooking oil

8 (6 oz.) cans tomato paste

1 tsp. sweet basil

1 Tbsp. oregano

$1^1/_2$ c. sugar

4 Tbsp. salt

Cook tomatoes and garlic together; put through a sieve. Chop onions and peppers; cook in oil for 30 minutes. Add to the tomatoes. Add remaining ingredients. Simmer together until it comes to a boil. Fill jars; seal.

Fannie Troyer, Quilt Binder

Pizza Sauce

$^1/_2$ bushel ripe tomatoes

3 lb. onions

4 hot peppers or

   $1^1/_2$ tsp. red pepper

2 c. vegetable oil

1 Tbsp. basil leaves

1 Tbsp. oregano

$^1/_2$ c. sugar

$^1/_2$ c. salt

4 (12 oz.) cans tomato paste

Cook tomatoes and onions for $2^1/_2$-3 hours; put through a sieve. Add peppers, oil, basil, oregano, sugar, and salt. Boil for 1 hour, then add tomato paste. Bring to a boil. Pack into hot jars; seal. Yields 20 pints.

Susan Yoder, Quilter

Mariner's Star

By the mighty ocean, a quiet lake, or a raging river, the Mariner's Star quilt is a favorite for people who enjoy water.

It is a nautical quilt with chains, anchors, and ocean waves quilted in the pattern of chain anchors.

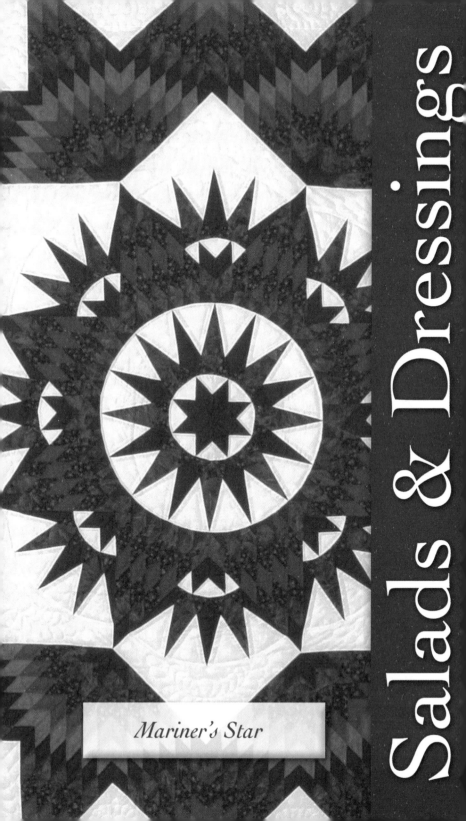

Mariner's Star

Salads & Dressings

Broccoli Salad

1 head broccoli	8 slices bacon
1 sm. head cauliflower	2 c. shredded cheddar cheese
1 med. onion, chopped	

Dressing:

³/₄ c. sour cream	³/₄ c. salad dressing
¹/₂ c. sugar	¹/₂ tsp. salt

Cut up vegetables. Fry bacon; cool and chop. Mix together. Toss with cheese and dressing.

Amanda Yoder, Quilter

Taco Salad

1 head lettuce, chopped	1 lg. onion, chopped
1 lb. hamburger	4 med. tomatoes, diced
8 oz. cheddar cheese	1 pkg. taco-flavored chips
1 sm. can kidney beans	1 pkg. taco seasoning

Dressing:

8 oz. Thousand Island dressing	1 Tbsp. taco sauce
¹/₃ c. sugar	1 Tbsp. taco seasoning

Brown hamburger. Add taco seasoning, reserving 1 Tbsp. for dressing. Select a large bowl, allowing enough room to toss at serving time. Layer salad ingredients in bowl, starting with the lettuce and ending with the cheese. Cover and refrigerate. At serving time, toss salad with dressing and chips.

Mrs. Steven Yoder

Taco Seasoning Salad

1 can refried beans	onions
2 c. sour cream	green peppers
8 oz. cream cheese	tomatoes
1 pkg. taco seasoning	cheese
¹/₂ jar taco sauce or salsa	Doritos
lettuce	

Put refried beans on bottom of plate. Mix sour cream and cream cheese with taco seasoning. Spread over beans. Top with taco sauce and remaining ingredients, except Doritos. Serve with Doritos, like a dip.

Ada Marie Miller, Quilt Piecer

Potato Salad

12 c. shredded potatoes   ¹/₂ med. onion, chopped
12 hard-boiled eggs   1¹/₂ c. chopped celery

Dressing:
3 c. salad dressing   6 Tbsp. mustard (scant)
¹/₄ c. vinegar   2¹/₂ c. sugar
4 tsp. salt (scant)   ¹/₂ c. milk

   Prepare a day before serving. Yields 3 qt.

Mrs. Effie Hershberger, Quilter
Mattie Hershberger, Quilter

Potato Salad

12 c. cooked, shredded potatoes   1¹/₂ c. chopped celery
12 hard-boiled eggs, chopped   shredded carrots
¹/₂ onion, chopped

Dressing:
3 c. salad dressing   2¹/₂ c. sugar
6 tsp. prepared mustard   ¹/₄ c. vinegar
2 tsp. salt   ¹/₂ c. milk

   Combine dressing ingredients and pour over other ingredients. Good
when mixed several days before serving.

Mrs. Malinda Miller, Quilt Marker

Potato Salad

12 c. shredded potatoes   1¹/₂ c. chopped celery
18 eggs   2 med. onions
2 c. macaroni

Dressing:
3 c. salad dressing   ¹/₄ c. vinegar
4 Tbsp. mustard   2¹/₂ c. sugar
4 tsp. salt   ¹/₂ c. milk

   Can be made a few days before serving.

Mrs. Eli E. Zook, Quilter

Cole Slaw

1 lg. head cabbage
$^1/_2$ c. chopped onion
1 Tbsp. celery seed
$^1/_2$ c. vinegar
2 c. sugar

1 c. sliced celery
1 green pepper, chopped
2 tsp. salt
$^1/_2$ tsp. mustard seed

Mix and let set overnight.

Fannie Troyer, Quilt Binder

Triple Orange Salad

1 sm. pkg. orange Jell-O
1 sm. pkg. instant vanilla pudding
1 sm. pkg. tapioca pudding

$2^1/_2$ c. cold water
1 can mandarin oranges
2 c. Cool Whip

Combine Jell-O, puddings, and cold water. Bring to a boil; cook for 3 minutes. Cool. Add remaining ingredients.

Sadie Yoder, Quilt Binder

Cool Whip Salad

1 can crushed pineapple
1 c. sugar
6 Tbsp. cold water
2 pkg. gelatin
1 c. salad dressing

1 carton Cool Whip
$1^1/_2$ c. cottage cheese
1 c. chopped celery
$^1/_2$ c. chopped nuts, optional

In a large bowl, combine pineapple and sugar. Bring cold water and gelatin to a boil. Pour over pineapple and sugar. Let set until thickened. Add remaining ingredients.

Anna Hershberger, Quilter

Cream Cheese Salad

2 pkg. orange Jell-O
8 oz. cream cheese
1 can crushed pineapple

1 c. cream, whipped
1 c. sugar
1 tsp. vanilla

Prepare 1 pkg. Jell-O. Pour half in bottom of a flat dish and let set. Prepare remaining Jell-O for top. Mix other pkg. of Jell-O with 1 cup hot water; let cool. Add pineapple, whipped cream, cream cheese, sugar, and vanilla to thickened Jell-O in dish; let set. Add remaining Jell-O to the top.

Mrs. Mary N. Zook, Quilter

Rainbow Jell-O Salad

2 c. sour cream
1 pkg. cherry Jell-O
1 pkg. lemon Jell-O
1 pkg. orange Jell-O

1 pkg. lime Jell-O
1 pkg. strawberry Jell-O
5 c. boiling water
1 1/2 c. cold water

Mix 1 c. boiling water with each package of Jell-O. Mix 1/2 c. of each Jell-O with 1/3 c. sour cream. Add 1/4 c. water to each remaining Jell-O. Layer in a clear glass dish, beginning with cherry/sour cream Jell-O, then plain cherry Jell-O. Refrigerate each layer to set before adding the next layer. End with the strawberry layers. You will have 10 layers.

Wilma Yoder, Quilt Piecer

French Dressing

2 sm. onions
2 c. vegetable oil
1 1/2 c. sugar
1 c. vinegar
1/2 c. ketchup

4 1/2 tsp. Worcestershire sauce
1 Tbsp. salt
1 Tbsp. prepared mustard
1 Tbsp. paprika
1 1/2 tsp. garlic powder

In a blender, process all ingredients until smooth and thickened. Cover and refrigerate for at least 1 hour. Shake well before serving.

Mrs. Floyd Yoder

French Salad Dressing

2 c. sugar
2 c. Wesson oil
3/4 c. ketchup
1/3 c. vinegar
1/2 c. chopped onion

1 c. salad dressing
2 tsp. Worcestershire sauce
salt
garlic salt
seasoning salt

This will keep for a long time. Yields 6 cups.

Wilma Yoder, Quilt Piecer

Tossed Salad Dressing

1 Tbsp. salad dressing
2 Tbsp. grated onion
1/2 c. ketchup
1/2 c. sugar
Beat together.

1/2 c. vegetable oil
1/4 c. vinegar
1 tsp. salt
1 Tbsp. lemon juice, optional

Mrs. John E. Weaver

ABOUT THE QUILT
Pineapple Delight

Personally, this is one of my favorites. It doesn't take lots of different fabrics—two main ones and one fill-in. The Pineapple Delight makes me think pineapple pudding, pineapple delight, and pineapple cake, featured on the following pages.

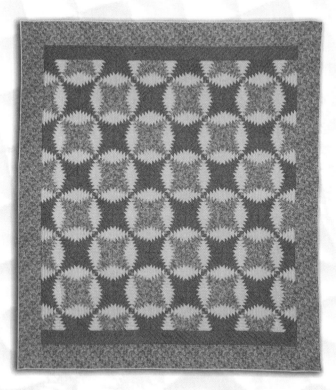

Desserts

Pineapple Delight

Pineapple Pudding

1 (16 oz.) can pineapple chunks
½ c. whipped topping
2 Tbsp. flour
salt

2 eggs
1 c. sugar
2 oranges
24 marshmallows

Drain pineapple. Heat juice with sugar, flour, and eggs; bring to boil. Cool. Combine with remaining ingredients. Chill for 1 hour.

Sara Yoder

Pinescotch Pudding

2 eggs, beaten
1 c. crushed pineapple
1 c. sugar
1 c. nuts

¾ c. flour
1 tsp. baking powder
¼ tsp. salt

Sauce:
¼ c. butter
¼ c. pineapple juice
¼ c. water

1 c. brown sugar
1 egg

Combine eggs, pineapple, sugar, and nuts. Add flour, baking powder, and salt. Bake at 350° until done. Cook sauce ingredients together; cool. Cut cake apart. Layer cake, sauce, and 2 c. whipped topping.

Sara Yoder

Pineapple Delight

1 lb. marshmallows
½ c. milk
1 c. crushed pineapple

1 c. whipped topping
1 tsp. vanilla
10 graham crackers, crushed

Heat marshmallows and milk in double boiler until melted. Add pineapple, vanilla, and whipped topping. Put graham cracker crumbs in bottom of dish, reserving some for the top. Pour pineapple mixture over crust. Sprinkle remaining crumbs on top.

Sara Yoder

Pinescotch Pudding

¾ c. flour
½ tsp. salt
1 tsp. baking powder
1 c. sugar

2 eggs, beaten
1 tsp. vanilla
1 c. chopped nuts
1 c. crushed pineapple, drained

Sauce:

¹/₄ c. water
¹/₄ c. butter, melted
1 c. brown sugar

1 Tbsp. flour
1 egg, beaten
¹/₄ c. pineapple juice

Sift dry ingredients. Combine eggs and sugar, beating until thick and ivory colored. Add vanilla; fold in pineapple and nuts. Gently fold in dry ingredients. Pour into a well-greased 12x8 pan. Bake at 325° for 30-35 minutes. Cool; cut into squares. For sauce, combine ingredients in a saucepan and bring to a boil, stirring constantly. Add vanilla. Cover and chill until ready to serve. Pour over squares. Top with whipped cream.

Iva, Quilter

Pineapple Cake

1¹/₂ c. sugar
¹/₂ c. lard
1 c. cold water
1 sm. can crushed pineapple

2¹/₂ c. flour
3 egg whites, beaten
3 tsp. baking powder

Lizzie Yoder, Quilt Piecer

Apricot Salad

2 c. water
¹/₃ c. sugar
2 pkg. apricot Jell-O
1 sm. can crushed pineapple

1 c. chopped celery
3 oz. cream cheese
2 c. whipped topping

Heat water; add sugar. Add to Jell-O. Add remaining ingredients. Make a day ahead and pour into a mold.

Susan Miller

Cream Cheese Pudding

graham cracker crumbs
8 oz. cream cheese
powdered sugar

whipped topping
1 can pineapple rings
1 pkg. orange Jell-O

Put graham cracker crumbs in bottom of pan. Combine cream cheese, powdered sugar, and whipped topping. Spread over graham cracker crust. Layer pineapple rings on top. Mix Jell-O according to directions on package. Allow to set slightly, then pour over pineapple rings.

Mattie A. Miller, Quilter

Ribbon Salad

1 pkg. lemon Jell-O
1 pkg. lime Jell-O
1 pkg. raspberry Jell-O
3 c. boiling water
1 c. miniature marshmallows

1 1/2 c. cold water
2 (3 oz.) pkg. cream cheese, softened
1/2 c. mayonnaise
1 c. whipped cream
1 (20.5 oz) can crushed pineapple

Dissolve Jell-O flavors separately, using 1 c. boiling water for each. Stir marshmallows into lemon Jell-O; set aside. Add 3/4 c. cold water to lime Jell-O; pour into a 9x13 pan. Chill until set, but not firm. Add 3/4 c. cold water to raspberry Jell-O; set aside at room temperature. Add cream cheese to lemon mixture; beat until blended. Chill until slightly thickened, then blend in mayonnaise, whipped cream, and pineapple. Chill until very thick. Spoon gently over lime Jell-O. Chill until set, but not firm. Meanwhile, chill raspberry Jell-O until thickened. Pour over lemon mixture. Chill until firm.

Mrs. Christ Miller Jr., Quilt Piecer

Orange Dessert

2 c. water
3/4 c. sugar
2 Tbsp. clear jel
1/3 c. orange Jell-O

1 1/2 whipped topping
pineapple
mandarin oranges

Bring water and sugar to a boil. Thicken with clear jel and a little water. Add Jell-O. Cool. When thickened, add remaining ingredients.

Anna Hershberger, Quilter

Orange Jell-O Dessert

4 c. water
1/2 c. small pearl tapioca
pinch salt
1 pkg. orange Jell-O

1/2 c. sugar
mandarin oranges
Cool Whip

Combine water, tapioca, and salt. Cook for 10 minutes, stirring often. Remove from heat. Add Jell-O and sugar; cool. Stir in oranges and Cool Whip.

Sara Yoder

Orange Tapioca Pudding

1 pkg. orange Jell-O
1 pkg. vanilla pudding (to cook)
1 pkg. tapioca pudding
3 c. boiling water
12 oz. Cool Whip
1 can mandarin oranges

Combine Jell-O, puddings, and boiling water; bring to a boil. Cool. Add Cool Whip and oranges. If too thick, add some juice.

Esther Hershberger, Quilter

Cherry Berries on a Cloud

Meringue Shell:
3 egg whites
$^1/_4$ tsp. cream of tartar
$^3/_4$ c. sugar

Topping:
8 oz. cream cheese
$^1/_2$ c. sugar
$^1/_2$ tsp. vanilla
1 c. whipped topping
1 c. marshmallows

Heat oven to 275°. Cover baking sheet with heavy brown paper. Beat egg whites and cream of tartar until foamy. Beat in sugar, 1 Tbsp. at a time. Continue beating until stiff and glossy. Do not underbeat. On brown paper, shape meringue into a 9" circle, building up sides. Bake for $1^1/_2$ hours. Turn off oven. Leave meringue in the oven for 1 hour with the door closed. Remove from oven; finish cooling meringue away from draft. Spoon topping into meringue shell. Top with your favorite fruit topping.

Mrs. Andrew A. Yoder, Quilt Piecer

Grape Jell-O Dessert

3 lg. pkg. grape Jell-O
1 c. powdered sugar
8 oz. cream cheese
1 c. Rich's topping, whipped
water

Dissolve 1 pkg. Jell-O in 2 c. boiling water. Add 2 c. cold water and pour into Tupperware or glass pan. Let set. Dissolve 1 pkg. Jell-O in 3 c. boiling water. Combine cream cheese and powdered sugar. Mix well; add whipped topping. When Jell-O is set, add to cream cheese mixture and spread on top of first Jell-O layer. Dissolve remaining pkg. Jell-O in 2 c. boiling water. Add 2 c. cold water and let set until syrupy. Pour over cream cheese mixture. Keep refrigerated.

Freda Miller

Grape Dessert

1/3 c. grape Jell-O	1 Tbsp. sour cream
1 c. hot water	1/4 c. powdered sugar
4 oz. cream cheese	2 c. whipped topping

Mix grape Jell-O and hot water; cool. Mix cream cheese, sour cream, powdered sugar, and whipped topping. Spread in a dish. Pour cooled grape Jell-O over top.

Mattie Troyer, Quilter

Rhubarb Crumbles

3 c. diced rhubarb	1/3 c. brown sugar
2 Tbsp. orange juice	2/3 c. sifted flour
3/4 c. sugar	1/8 tsp. salt
1/4 tsp. cinnamon	1/4 tsp. soda
1 Tbsp. butter	2/3 c. quick oats
1/4 c. butter, melted	

Arrange rhubarb in a greased baking pan. Combine orange juice, sugar, and cinnamon; sprinkle over rhubarb. Dot with 1 Tbsp. butter. Combine melted butter, brown sugar, flour, salt, and soda. Mix with quick oats. Spread over rhubarb. Bake at 375° for 40 minutes. Serve warm with cream or milk.

Mrs. John E. Weaver

Apple Crisp

4 c. sliced apples	3/4 tsp. cinnamon
3/4 c. brown sugar	1/3 c. soft margarine
1/2 c. flour	1/4 tsp. baking powder
1/2 c. rolled oats	

Combine flour, oats, cinnamon, margarine, and baking powder. Mix until crumbly. Place apples in a baking pan. Top with brown sugar and crumbs. Bake for 30 minutes or until apples are soft.

Emma Schlabach, Quilter

Apple Dumplings

Syrup:

1 c. sugar	2 c. water
3 Tbsp. butter	1/4 tsp. cinnamon

Make a pastry like a pie crust, using milk instead of water. Roll out and cut into 7" squares. Pare and core a medium tart apple for each dumpling. Fill cavities of apples with a mixture of ½ c. sugar and 1½ tsp. cinnamon. Dot with butter. Fold crust over apple and seal. Place in baking dish. Pour hot syrup around dumplings. Bake immediately at 425° for 40-45 minutes.

Fannie Yoder, Quilter

Apple Dumplings

Dough:

2 c. flour	⅔ c. margarine
2½ tsp. baking powder	½ c. milk
½ tsp. salt	6 apples, peeled, halved

Sauce:

2 c. brown sugar	¼ c. butter
2 c. water	½ tsp. cinnamon

Wrap apple halves in dough and put in cake pan. Pour sauce over all and bake at 350° for 1 hour. Delicious with ice cream or with plain milk. Serve warm.

Anna Yoder, Quilter · Mrs. Ella Keim, Quilt Piecer

Pumpkin Roll

3 eggs	2 tsp. cinnamon
1 c. sugar	1 tsp. ginger
⅔-¾ c. canned pumpkin	½ tsp. nutmeg
¾ c. all-purpose flour	½ tsp. salt
1 tsp. baking powder	

Filling:

8 oz. cream cheese, softened	1 c. powdered sugar
4 Tbsp. margarine	1 tsp. vanilla

Combine eggs and sugar, beating well. Add pumpkin, mixing until blended. In a separate bowl, combine dry ingredients. Add to egg mixture, mixing well. Spread batter into wax paper-lined 10x15 jellyroll pan. Bake at 375° for 15 minutes. Remove from pan. Let cool for 15 minutes. Place on clean tea towel. Cool 10 minutes longer. From short side, roll cake up in towel. Set aside. Meanwhile, prepare filling. Beat together cream cheese and margarine. Stir in powdered sugar and vanilla, blending until smooth. Unroll cake; place on plastic wrap. Evenly spread filling over cake. Roll up and cover with plastic wrap. Chill for 2 hours.

Nettie Yoder, Quilter · Ada Marie Miller

Date Pudding

1 c. dates	1 egg
1 c. hot water	1 tsp. vanilla
1 c. sugar	1/2 c. nuts
1 Tbsp. butter	2 c. cream, whipped
1 1/2 c. flour	pinch salt
1 tsp. soda	

Pour boiling water over dates; let set 5 minutes. Cream sugar, butter, egg, and salt together; add date mixture, flour, and soda. Stir in vanilla. Bake at 375° for 30-35 minutes. When cool, cut cake into small squares. Fold squares into whipped cream. Chill.

Frances H. Gingerich, Quilter

Fluff Pudding

2 egg yolks, beaten	2 egg whites, beaten
1/2 c. milk	1 c. cream, whipped
1 c. sugar	vanilla
1 pkg. gelatin	1/3 c. butter
1/3 c. cold water	16 graham crackers, crushed

Combine egg yolks, milk, and sugar; bring to a boil. Cook for 1 minute, stirring constantly. Dissolve gelatin in cold water. Pour this into hot mixture; let set until cool. Add egg whites, whipped cream, and vanilla. Combine butter and graham cracker crumbs. Put in pan, then pour gelatin mixture over top.

Jimmy Carter Pudding

Layer 1:

1 c. flour	1/2 c. butter
2/3 c. salted peanuts	

Layer 2:

1/3 c. peanut butter	1 c. powdered sugar
8 oz. cream cheese	1 c. whipped cream

Layer 3:

1 pkg. instant chocolate pudding	2 3/4 c. milk
1 pkg. instant vanilla pudding	

Layer 4:

whipped cream	chopped peanuts

Mix flour, peanuts, and butter. Press into a 9x13 pan. Bake at 350° for 20 minutes; cool. Combine peanut butter, cream cheese, powdered sugar, and whipped cream. Spread over crust. Combine puddings and milk. Spread over cream cheese filling. Top with whipped cream; sprinkle with chopped peanuts.

Lucinda Yoder, Quilt Appliqués

Chocolate Peanut Torte

2 c. vanilla wafer crumbs
1/3 c. butter, melted
1 c. peanuts, finely
    chopped, divided
8 oz. cream cheese, softened
1 c. powdered sugar

1/2 c. peanut butter
4 c. whipped topping, divided
3 c. cold milk
2 pkg. instant chocolate pudding
1 (1.55 oz.) milk chocolate
    candy bar, grated

Combine wafer crumbs, butter, and 2/3 c. peanuts. Press into an ungreased 9x13 baking dish. Bake at 350° for 8-10 minutes or until lightly browned. Cool. In a mixing bowl, beat cream cheese, sugar, and peanut butter until smooth. Fold in 2 c. whipped topping. Spread over crust. In a mixing bowl, beat milk and pudding mixes on low for 2 minutes. Carefully spread over cream cheese layer. Cover and refrigerate for 4-6 hours. Just before serving, carefully spread remaining topping over the pudding layer. Sprinkle with grated chocolate and the remaining peanuts.

LeAnna Troyer

Butterfinger Dessert

1 1/2 pkg. graham crackers, crushed
3/4 c. margarine
1 pkg. instant vanilla pudding
1 pkg. instant butterscotch pudding

2 c. milk
1 qt. vanilla ice cream
1 sm. carton Cool Whip
4 Butterfinger candy bars

Combine cracker crumbs and margarine. Press 3/4 of mixture into a 9x13 pan. Combine pudding and milk. Add ice cream. Beat until smooth. Pour over crumbs and refrigerate for 1 hour. Spread with Cool Whip. Crush candy bars and add to remaining crumbs. Sprinkle on top.

Lydia Yoder, Quilter

Butterfinger Dessert

1½ pkg. graham crackers, crushed 2 c. milk
30 soda crackers, crushed 8 oz. Cool Whip
¾ c. margarine, melted 1 qt. vanilla ice cream, softened
2 pkg. instant vanilla pudding 3 Butterfinger candy bars, crushed

Combine crackers and margarine. Mix; press ¾ of it into a 9x13 pan. Beat pudding and milk together; add ice cream. Spread over crackers. Top with Cool Whip. Mix candy bars with remaining crumbs. Sprinkle on top.

Rosie Hershberger, Quilt Piecer

Cookie Pudding

1 lb. Oreo cookies, crushed ½ c. butter, melted
Filling:
1 pkg. instant vanilla pudding 3½ c. milk
8 oz. cream cheese 1 c. whipped cream

Mix the cookie crumbs and butter. Set this in a dish. Mix pudding, cream cheese, and milk. Spread over crust. Top with whipped cream.

Miss Mary E. Zook, Quilter

Oreo Pudding

2 pkg. vanilla pudding 8 oz. cream cheese, softened
1½ c. whipped cream 1 (20 oz.) pkg. Oreo cookies

Cook pudding according to directions on package; cool. Beat cream cheese; fold in whipped cream. Fold into cooled pudding. Crush cookies. In a shallow pan, layer half of the cookie crumbs, pudding mixture, then remaining cookie crumbs.

Mattie Hershberger, Quilter

Frozen Strawberry Dessert

Ritz cracker crumbs 1 tsp. salt
4 egg whites, beaten 1 tsp. vanilla
1½ c. sugar 4 c. frozen strawberries
2 Tbsp. lemon juice 2 c. whipped topping

Put cracker crumbs in a pan. With wire whip, combine egg whites, sugar, lemon juice, salt, vanilla, and strawberries. Fold in whipped topping; pour over crumbs. Sprinkle some cracker crumbs on top; freeze.

Mrs. Dan C. Yoder, Quilt Piecer

Caramel Ice Cream Dessert

$^3/_4$ c. oatmeal
$^1/_2$-$^3/_4$ c. brown sugar
2 c. flour
$^3/_4$ c. chopped pecans

1 c. margarine
caramel ice cream topping
$^1/_2$ gal. vanilla ice cream

Combine oatmeal, brown sugar, flour, pecans, and margarine. Bake at 350° for 20-25 minutes, stirring occasionally; cool. Put half of crumbs in a pan. Top with half of the caramel topping. Spread softened ice cream on top. Drizzle with remaining caramel topping. Cover with remaining crumbs. Freeze. This stays good in the freezer for several days.

Wilma Yoder, Quilt Piecer

Homemade Ice Cream

7 c. milk, scalded
1$^1/_2$ c. sugar
pinch of salt
vanilla
1 c. cold milk
1 pkg. unflavored gelatin

4 egg yolks, beaten
1 c. sugar
1 lg. pkg. instant vanilla pudding
2 c. half and half
1 c. cream

Combine scalded milk, sugar, salt, and vanilla. Dissolve gelatin in cold milk. Pour into first milk mixture. Add remaining ingredients. Put into ice cream freezer. Freeze.

Ada Marie Miller

Homemade Ice Cream

6 c. milk, scalded
8 egg yolks, beaten
$^1/_2$ c. flour
2 pkg. vanilla pudding (to cook)
1 c. sugar
1 c. brown sugar
$^1/_4$ tsp. salt

1 Tbsp. vanilla
4 egg whites, beaten
$^1/_2$ c. brown sugar
2 pkg. Knox gelatin
$^1/_2$ c. cold milk
2 c. whipping cream

Combine milk, egg yolks, flour, pudding, sugars, salt, and vanilla. Heat until thick; remove from heat. Beat egg whites; add $^1/_2$ c. brown sugar. Add to first mixture. Dissolve gelatin in $^1/_2$ c. cold milk; add. Slightly whip the whipping cream. Add, then pour into ice cream freezer can. Add milk to 3" from the top of the can. Freeze.

Sara Yoder

ABOUT THE QUILT

Multi-Fan Star

Our daughter, Miriam, pieced this stars and fans quilt.
It has a star pattern in a Log Cabin design. Star patterns are always a favorite with people, so it is with this
one.

Cookies

Multi-Fan Star

Chocolate Chip Pudding Cookies

2¼ c. flour
1 c. butter or margarine, softened
¾ c. brown sugar
1 tsp. vanilla
1 pkg. chocolate chips

1 tsp. baking soda
¼ c. sugar
1 pkg. instant vanilla pudding
2 eggs
1 c. chopped nuts

Mix flour and baking soda. Combine butter, sugars, pudding mix, and vanilla in a large bowl; beat until smooth and creamy. Beat in eggs. Gradually add flour mixture, then chips and nuts. Batter will be stiff. Drop by rounded teaspoonful onto ungreased cookie sheets. Bake at 375° for 8-10 minutes. Yields about 7 doz.

Fannie Yoder, Quilter

Chocolate Chip Cookies

2½ c. sugar
2½ c. brown sugar
2 c. vegetable oil
8 eggs
2 tsp. vanilla

8 c. bread flour
4 tsp. soda
1 tsp. baking powder
1 tsp. salt
2 c. chocolate chips

Cream together sugars and oil. Add eggs and vanilla. Stir in dry ingredients. Add chocolate chips last.

Nettie Yoder, Quilter

Chocolate Chip Cookies

2 c. brown sugar
1 c. sugar
2 tsp. salt
2 c. shortening
1 tsp. vanilla

4 tsp. soda
6 eggs
4 tsp. cream of tartar
7 c. flour
2-3 pkg. chocolate chips

Ada Zook, age 12, Quilter

Chocolate Chip Cookies

2¼ c. all-purpose flour
1 tsp. baking powder
1 c. soft margarine
¼ c. sugar
¾ c. brown sugar

1 tsp. vanilla
1 pkg. instant vanilla pudding
2 eggs
1 pkg. chocolate chips

Ina Yoder

Chocolate Chip Cookies

1½ c. sugar
1½ c. brown sugar
1 c. shortening
4 eggs, beaten
5-6 c. flour

5 Tbsp. hot water
2 tsp. soda
4 tsp. vanilla
½ tsp. salt
1 pkg. chocolate chips

Bake at 350° for 10 minutes.

Mrs. Ura A. Troyer, Quilter

Chocolate Chip Cookies

3 c. margarine
2 c. brown sugar
1 c. sugar
2 pkg. instant vanilla pudding

6 eggs
3 tsp. soda
4 c. chocolate chips
7 c. flour

Laura Troyer, Quilt Piecer

Soft Batch Chocolate Chip Cookies

5½ c. Gold Medal flour
3 tsp. soda dissolved in
    3 Tbsp. hot water
3 c. brown sugar

1½ c. margarine
3 tsp. vanilla
3 eggs
1 c. chocolate chips

Drop onto cookie sheets and bake at 350°.

Arlene Hershberger, Quilt Piecer

Chewy Chocolate Chip Bars

1 chocolate or yellow cake mix
1 egg
1⅓ c. coconut
¾ c. nuts

1 can sweetened condensed milk
1 tsp. vanilla
1 pkg. chocolate chips

Mix until soft and crumbly. Press into a 9x13 baking pan. Bake at 350° for 30-40 minutes.

Lydia Yoder, Quilter

$400 Cookies

2 c. margarine	5 c. oatmeal
2 c. sugar	4 c. flour
2 c. brown sugar	1 (8 oz.) chocolate candy bar, cut up
4 eggs	4 c. chocolate chips
2 tsp. soda	3 c. nuts, optional
1/2 tsp. salt	

Mix together. Bake at 350° for 10-12 minutes. Do not overbake.

Mrs. Floyd Yoder, Quilt Piecer

Children's Favorite Cookies

1/2 c. butter or lard	1 c. sugar
1 c. brown sugar	2 c. flour
2 eggs	2 c. oatmeal
1 c. coconut	1 tsp. baking powder
1 tsp. soda	1 tsp. salt
2 tsp. vanilla	

Bake at 350°.

Sevilla Swartzentruber, Quilter

Coconut Oatmeal Cookies

2 c. lard	2 tsp. soda
2 c. brown sugar	2 tsp. baking powder
2 c. sugar	1 c. fine coconut
4 eggs	2 tsp. vanilla
6 c. oatmeal	1/2 tsp. coconut flavoring
3 1/2 c. flour	1 c. nuts, optional

Mix in order given. Make walnut-sized balls and press flat, or shape into rolls and chill overnight, then slice. Bake until nicely browned.

Katie J. Zook, Quilter

Sunny Field Oatmeal Cookies

2 c. brown sugar	2 tsp. maple flavoring
1 c. sugar	2 tsp. soda
4 c. flour	2 tsp. salt
4 c. quick oats	2 tsp. baking powder
4 eggs, beaten	4 Tbsp. milk
4 tsp. vanilla	1 1/4 c. shortening

Beat sugars, shortening, eggs, vanilla, maple flavoring, and milk. Mix flour, soda, baking powder, and salt. Add oats; mix well. Shape into rolls, then slice. Bake at 350°.

Mrs. Andy J. Swartzentruber, Quilter

Monster Cookies

12 eggs	8 tsp. soda
4 c. brown sugar	2 c. butter
4 c. sugar	18 c. oatmeal
1 tsp. vanilla	1 lb. chocolate chips
1 tsp. Karo	

Mix in order given. Drop by teaspoonsful onto cookie sheets. Bake at 350°. Do not overbake.

Lizzie Yoder, Quilt Piecer

Monster Cookies

$3/4$ c. margarine	$2^1/2$ tsp. soda
1 c. sugar	4 c. oatmeal
1 c. brown sugar	$1/2$ lb. M&M's
4 eggs	12 oz. chocolate chips
1 lb. peanut butter	

Cream together margarine and sugars. Add eggs and peanut butter; beat well. Add rest of ingredients, adding M&M's and chocolate chips last. More oatmeal may be necessary to make a stiff dough. Form balls and roll in powdered sugar. Bake at 350° for 10 minutes. Do not overbake.

Nettie Yoder, Quilter

Spellbinder Cookies

3 c. flour	2 c. rolled oats
3 tsp. baking powder	2 c. fine coconut
2 tsp. soda	1 c. crushed corn flakes
3 c. brown sugar	$1^1/2$-2 c. nuts
2 c. margarine	2 c. chocolate chips
2 eggs	

Frosting:

2 Tbsp. butter or margarine, melted	1 Tbsp. hot water or more
1 c. powdered sugar	vanilla

Mrs. Ella Keim, Quilt Piecer

Soft Sugar Cookies

2 c. margarine, creamed
1 c. brown sugar
2 c. sugar
4 eggs
2 c. cream

8-10 c. Thesco flour
1/2 tsp. salt
2 tsp. soda
6 tsp. baking powder

Bake at 350°. Do not overbake or they won't be soft. For sandwich cookies, put filling between two cookies.

Mrs. Susan Kauffman, Quilter · Esther Hershberger, Quilter

Sour Cream Cookies

4 1/2 c. brown sugar
5 eggs, beaten
3 c. sour cream or milk
1 1/2 tsp. salt
flour

1/2 c. margarine
3 tsp. soda
6 tsp. baking powder
2 tsp. vanilla

Dissolve soda in sour milk. Combine all ingredients, adding flour until dough is the right consistency.

Mrs. Nelson E. Weaver, Quilter

Fresh Orange Cookies

1 1/2 c. flour
1/2 tsp. baking soda
1/4 tsp. salt
1/2 c. butter, softened
1/2 c. sugar
1/2 c. brown sugar
1 egg

1 unpeeled orange, finely chopped
1/2 c. chopped walnuts
1-2 Tbsp. freshly-squeezed
  orange juice
1 c. powdered sugar
1 Tbsp. butter, softened
1 Tbsp. freshly grated orange peel

Sift together flour, baking soda, and salt in a large bowl. Cream 1/2 c. butter and sugars. Add egg. Chop the orange in a blender or food processor or by hand to equal 3/4 c. chopped fruit. Add; beat well. Gradually blend in flour mixture. Stir in walnuts. Cover; chill for 1 hour or longer. Drop dough by teaspoonful onto lightly greased cookie sheets. Bake at 375° for 10-12 minutes. Remove and cool on wire racks. Combine powdered sugar, fresh orange juice, butter, and orange peel. Spread glaze over cooled cookies. Yields about 4 dozen.

Mrs. Mose Keim, Quilter

Orange Cookies

1 c. soft margarine
2 c. sugar
3 eggs, beaten
1 c. sour milk or buttermilk
grated rind of 1 orange

¹/₄ c. orange juice
6 c. sifted flour
1 tsp. baking soda
2 tsp. baking powder

Frosting:
1 orange, finely ground
2 Tbsp. butter

powdered sugar

Cream together margarine and sugar. Add eggs, sour milk, orange rind, and juice. Sift together dry ingredients; add to first mixture. Drop by teaspoonsful onto cookie sheets. Bake at 350°. For frosting, combine ingredients, adding powdered sugar until spreadable.

Sara Yoder

Buttermilk Cookies

6 c. brown sugar
2 c. sugar
3 c. lard
12 eggs
salt
vanilla

4 tsp. baking powder
4 tsp. cream of tartar
3 c. milk
8 tsp. soda
flour

Dissolve soda in milk. Mix all ingredients together. Add flour until you reach the desired consistency. Bake at 350°.

Mrs. Malinda Miller, Quilt Marker

Buttermilk Cookies

1 c. sugar
1 c. brown sugar
1 c. butter or lard
3 eggs
2 tsp. soda

2 tsp. baking powder
1 c. buttermilk
vanilla
3-4 c. flour

Mix all ingredients together. May use half bread flour if desired.

Mrs. Mary Troyer, Quilter

Cream Wafers

1/2 c. butter	1 c. brown sugar
2 eggs	2³/4 c. flour
1¹/2 tsp. vanilla	2 Tbsp. sweet cream
1/2 tsp. salt	1/3 tsp. cinnamon
2 squares chocolate, melted	

Filling:

4 Tbsp. butter	2 Tbsp. hot cream
2 c. powdered sugar	1 tsp. vanilla

Verna H. Gingerich, Quilter

Sandwich Cookies

2 c. brown sugar	1 tsp. salt
1 c. butter or margarine	3 tsp. cinnamon
4 eggs, beaten	2 tsp. vanilla
1/4 c. sour cream	5¹/2 c. flour
3 tsp. soda	

Filling:

1 c. butter or Crisco	3 tsp. vanilla
9 Tbsp. sour cream	9 c. powdered sugar

Mix all together; put in cookie press. Bake at 350° until lightly browned.

Linda Yoder, Quilt Piecer

Chocolate Sandwich Gobs

2 c. sugar	2 tsp. salt
1 c. margarine, melted	1 c. sour milk
2 eggs, beaten	2 tsp. baking soda
4 c. all-purpose flour	your favorite chocolate icing
1/2 c. cocoa	

Combine sugar, margarine, and beaten eggs in a large mixing bowl; mix well. Sift together flour, cocoa, and salt. Alternately add dry ingredients and sour milk. Add baking soda, mixing until combined. Drop by teaspoonsful onto cookie sheets. Bake at 350° for 10 minutes.

Ada, Quilter

Whoopie Cookies

2 c. brown sugar	2 tsp. vanilla
2 c. sugar	8¹/2 c. flour
2 c. lard	4 tsp. soda

4 whole eggs
4 egg yolks
2 c. buttermilk

2 tsp. baking powder
1 c. cocoa

Filling:
1 c. Crisco
4 Tbsp. milk
1 lb. powdered sugar

4 Tbsp. flour
2 tsp. vanilla
2 egg whites

Mrs. Eli E. Zook, Quilter

Gobs

1 c. sugar
1 c. brown sugar
$^1/_2$ c. margarine or Crisco
2 eggs
2 tsp. soda
$^1/_2$ tsp. salt
$^1/_2$ tsp. baking powder

$^1/_2$ c. cocoa
4 c. all-purpose flour
1 c. sour milk or
   1 c. sweet milk + 1 Tbsp. vinegar
1 tsp. vanilla
1 c. boiling water

Filling:
3 c. powdered sugar
$1^1/_2$ c. Crisco
5 Tbsp. milk

3 tsp. vanilla
3 egg whites, stiffly beaten

Cream together sugars, margarine, and eggs. Add dry ingredients. Add sour milk and vanilla. Add boiling water. Best if chilled for a few hours. For filling, cream togther Crisco, powdered sugar, milk, and vanilla, then add stiffly beaten egg whites. Beat all together.

Sarah Troyer, Quilt Piecer

Chocolate Twinkies

1 chocolate cake mix
1 pkg. instant chocolate pudding
1 c. water

4 eggs
$^1/_2$ c. salad oil

Filling:
3 egg whites
3 c. powdered sugar
3 tsp. vanilla

1 c. Crisco
6 Tbsp. milk

Mix and bake in a 9x13 pan; cool. Slice lengthwise and put filling between layers.

Freida Yoder, Quilter

S'mores Bars

3 c. graham cracker crumbs
3/4 c. butter, softened
1/3 c. sugar

3 c. miniature marshmallows
2 c. semisweet chocolate chips

Combine the cracker crumbs, butter, and sugar. Press half of the mixture into a 9x13 pan. Sprinkle with marshmallows and chocolate chips. Top with remaining crumbs. Press firmly. Bake at 375° for 10 minutes or less. Remove from oven and press top firmly with a spatula after slightly cooled. Cool completely. Cut into bars. Very good.

Mrs. Joe M. Miller

Oreo Cookies

1 white or yellow cake mix
2 eggs
2 Tbsp. water

2 Tbsp. vegetable oil
1/2 c. cocoa

Filling:
3 egg whites
3 tsp. vanilla
3 c. powdered sugar

1 1/2 c. Crisco
6 Tbsp. water

Mix ingredients together. Let set for 20 minutes. Shape into balls. Flatten with Nestlé Quik. Bake at 350° for 8 minutes; cool. Mix filling and spread between 2 cookies.

Arlene Hershberger, Quilt Piecer

Suzy Q's

1 chocolate cake mix
1 pkg. instant vanilla pudding
4 eggs

1 c. water
1/2 c. oil

Filling:
2 egg whites
2 c. powdered sugar
1/4 tsp. salt

2 tsp. vanilla
1 1/2 c. Crisco

Bake on 2 cookie sheet pans at 350° until done. Mix filling and spread between cakes.

Mattie A. Miller, Quilter

Chewy Brownie Cookies

1¹/₃ c. shortening
3 c. brown sugar
2 Tbsp. water
4 eggs
2 tsp. vanilla
1 c. nuts

3 c. all-purpose flour
²/₃ c. cocoa
1 tsp. salt
¹/₂ tsp. soda
2 c. chocolate chips

Cream together shortening, sugar, water, and vanilla. Beat in eggs. Stir in remaining ingredients until blended. Do not overbake. Delicious!

Susie J. Zook, Quilter

Peanut Butter Sandwich Cookies

³/₄ c. margarine
1 c. sugar
1 c. brown sugar
1 c. peanut butter
2 eggs

1 tsp. vanilla
2 tsp. soda
1 Tbsp. water
4 c. flour

Filling:
¹/₂ c. peanut butter
¹/₂ tsp. vanilla

milk
powdered sugar

Cream together margarine and sugars. Add peanut butter, eggs, and vanilla. Dissolve soda in water; add to mixture. Add flour. Bake at 350°. Mix filling; spread between 2 cookies.

Laura Yoder, Quilter

Peanut Butter Dream Bars

Crust:
2 c. quick oats
1¹/₂ c. flour
1 c. margarine, melted

1 tsp. soda
1 c. brown sugar
³/₄ tsp. salt

Additional Ingredients:
¹/₃ c. peanut butter
1 c. M&M's and chocolate chips

1 can sweetened condensed milk

Combine crust ingredients until crumbly. Set aside 1¹/₂ cups. Press remaining crumbs into a jellyroll pan. Bake at 350° for 10 minutes. Mix peanut butter and milk; spread over crust. Mix reserved crumbs with M&M's and chocolate chips. Sprinkle on top. Bake for 20 minutes longer.

Anna Yoder, Quilter

Eggless Peanut Butter Cookies

1 c. butter or lard	3 c. flour
1 c. peanut butter	1½ tsp. soda
1 c. brown sugar	3 Tbsp. hot water
1 c. white sugar	

Dissolve soda in hot water. Mix all ingredients together. Shape into balls; flatten with a potato masher. Bake. Very simple and good.

Mrs. Abe Byler, Quilter

Peanut Butter Strip Cookies

1 c. margarine	1 tsp. soda
1 c. brown sugar	½ tsp. salt
1 c. sugar	1 tsp. vanilla
2 eggs	2 c. flour
1 c. peanut butter	2 c. oatmeal

Filling:

6 oz. chocolate chips	1 Tbsp. margarine
½ can sweetened condensed milk	¼ tsp. salt
1 tsp. vanilla	

Icing:

¼ c. peanut butter	¼ c. margarine
1½ c. powdered sugar	milk

Cream together margarine and sugars; blend in remaining ingredients. Spread dough in a large, greased cookie sheet. Bake at 350° until done; cool. Mix filling; spread over cooled bars. Top with icing.

Effie Miller, Quilter

Peanut Butter Cookies

2 c. margarine	2 c. sugar
2 c. peanut butter	2 c. brown sugar
4 eggs	2 tsp. vanilla
4 tsp. baking soda	1 tsp. baking powder
1 tsp. salt	4½ c. flour

Shape into balls. Place on cookie sheet, and flatten with a potato masher.

Mrs. Nelson E. Weaver, Quilter

Gingerbread Cookies

$^1/_2$ c. sugar
$^1/_2$ c. butter or lard
1 egg
1 c. molasses
2$^1/_2$ c. flour
pinch salt

1 tsp. cinnamon
1 tsp. cloves
1 tsp. ginger
1$^1/_2$ tsp. soda
$^1/_2$ c. hot water

Dissolve soda in hot water. Mix all ingredients together.

Lizzie Yoder, Quilt Piecer

Sorghum Cookies

2$^1/_2$ c. sugar
2$^1/_2$ c. brown sugar
3 c. shortening
4 eggs
8 tsp. soda
1 c. milk

1 c. molasses
2 tsp. baking powder
4 tsp. cinnamon
1 tsp. salt
12 c. flour

Filling:
4 egg whites, beaten
8 c. powdered sugar, divided

2 c. Crisco

Dissolve soda in milk. Mix all ingredients together. Chill dough. Shape into balls; flatten with a glass dipped in white sugar. Bake. For filling, mix beaten egg whites with 4 c. powdered sugar. Add Crisco, then remaining powdered sugar.

Anna Yoder, Quilter

Granola Bars

2 pkg. miniature marshmallows
$^1/_4$ c. vegetable oil
$^1/_2$ c. peanut butter
$^3/_4$ c. butter
$^1/_4$ c. honey
4$^1/_2$ c. Rice Krispies

1 c. crushed graham crackers
chocolate chips
5 c. rolled oats
1 c. coconut
1 c. chopped nuts

Combine marshmallows, oil, peanut butter, butter, and honey; melt together, then add remaining ingredients. Add chocolate chips last so that they don't melt too much. Spread on cookie sheet; cut into bars.

Freda Miller

Granola Bars

2 (10½ oz.) pkg. marshmallows	1 c. coconut
¼ c. vegetable oil	3 pkg. graham crackers, crushed
¾ c. butter	chocolate chips
¼ c. honey	M&M's
¼ c. peanut butter	almonds
5 c. oatmeal	raisins
4½ c. Rice Krispies	

Over low heat, melt marshmallows, oil, butter, honey, and peanut butter. In a large mixing bowl, mix oatmeal, Rice Krispies, coconut, and graham cracker crumbs. Pour melted mixture over top; mix well. Add remaining ingredients. Spread into cookie sheet.

Mrs. Junior Weaver, Quilt Marker

Prune Cookies

1 c. brown sugar	3 c. flour
1 c. sugar	¾ c. chopped nuts
1 c. margarine	½ tsp. salt
1 c. cooked prunes, cut fine	1 tsp. soda
3 eggs	mixed spice

Combine sugars and shortening. Add eggs and prunes; mix well. Add dry ingredients and nuts. If dough is too stiff, add a little prune juice. Drop onto cookie sheets. Bake at 375°.

Mrs. Henry A. Hershberger, Quilt Piecer

Fruit Bars

3½ lb. flour	3 tsp. soda
2 lb. sugar	2 c. Brer Rabbit molasses
2 c. butter or margarine	5 eggs, well beaten
2 lb. seedless raisins	½ c. boiling water
½ c. water	

Cook raisins in ½ c. water. Dissolve soda in boiling water. Mix flour and sugar; add butter. Mix like pie dough. Add cooked raisins; mix again. Make a well and add all other ingredients. Brush top with beaten egg. Bake at 350°.

Fannie Troyer, Quilt Binder

Sour Cream Raisin Bars

Crumbs:

2 c. oatmeal	1 c. brown sugar
1 tsp. soda	1 tsp. vanilla
2 c. flour	1 c. margarine
1 tsp. baking powder	pinch salt

Filling:

2 c. sour cream	1 Tbsp. cornstarch
1 c. sugar	1 c. raisins
4 egg yolks	

Mix together crust ingredients. Set aside ⅔ c. of crumbs. Press remaining crumbs into a cookie sheet. Bake at 350° for 15 minutes; cool. In a saucepan, combine egg yolks, sugar, and cornstarch. Beat well, then add sour cream and raisins. Cook for 5 minutes, stirring constantly. Pour over crumbs. Sprinkle reserved crumbs on top. Bake for 20 minutes longer.

Mrs. Mose Keim, Quilter

Raisin-Filled Cookies

2 c. sugar	2 tsp. soda
2 eggs	4 tsp. cream of tartar
1 c. shortening	½ tsp. salt
1 c. milk	1 tsp. vanilla
4 c. flour	

Filling:

1½ c. raisins	1½ c. sugar
1½ c. water	1½ Tbsp. flour

Cream together shortening and sugar; add eggs and vanilla. Sift dry ingredients. Alternately add dry mixture and milk. Add enough flour to roll nicely. Grind raisins. Add remaining filling ingredients and bring to a boil. Roll out dough; cut into circles. Cut holes in circles used for tops. Put a teaspoon of filling on a circle; top with another circle. Pinch edges to seal. Bake at 350° for 10-12 minutes or until brown.

Emma Schlabach, Quilter

Thumbprint Cookies

¹/₂ c. butter	2 c. flour
¹/₂ c. shortening	¹/₂ tsp. salt
¹/₂ c. brown sugar	2 egg whites
2 egg yolks	finely chopped nuts
1 tsp. vanilla	

Mix shortening, sugar, egg yolks, and vanilla thoroughly. Add flour and salt; mix. Roll 1 tsp. dough into a ball. Dip into slightly beaten egg whites, then roll in nuts. Place 1" apart on ungreased cookie sheet. Press thumb gently into center. Bake for 10-12 minutes. Fill centers with frosting. Cream cheese icing is good.

Susan Yoder, Quilter

Double Chocolate Crumble Bars

¹/₂ c. margarine	2 Tbsp. cocoa
2 eggs	2 c. marshmallows
1 tsp. vanilla	1¹/₂ c. chocolate chips
³/₄ c. brown sugar	¹/₂ c. peanut butter
³/₄ c. flour	1¹/₂ c. Rice Krispies
¹/₄ tsp. baking powder	

Mix margarine, eggs, vanilla, brown sugar, flour, baking powder, and cocoa as you would for a cake. Spread into a 9x13 baking pan. Bake at 350° for 15-20 minutes. Spread marshmallows on top and return to oven for 2-3 minutes; cool. Melt chocolate chips and peanut butter in a double boiler. Stir in Rice Krispies. Spread on top of cooled bars. Cut into squares.

Emma, Quilter

Marble Squares

2¹/₂ c. margarine	7³/₄ c. flour
2¹/₄ c. sugar	1 tsp. soda
2¹/₄ c. brown sugar	2 tsp. baking powder
1¹/₂ tsp. salt	1¹/₂ c. chocolate chips
6 eggs	1 c. nut meats, optional
3 tsp. vanilla	

Cream margarine, sugars, eggs, and vanilla. Add flour, soda, baking powder, and salt. Spread into 2 greased jellyroll pans. Sprinkle chocolate chips on top. Put into a preheated oven for 2 minutes. Remove;

marbelize with a knife. Sprinkle nuts on top. Bake for 20 minutes. When cool, drizzle glaze on top.

Note: I like to mix the chocolate chips into the dough before spreading it into the jellyroll pans. They turn out like chocolate chip cookies, but are not nearly as time consuming.

Mrs. David A. Miller

Pecan Tarts

Crust:
$^1/_2$ c. margarine, softened   1 c. flour
3 oz. cream cheese, softened

Filling:
2 Tbsp. butter, melted $1^1/_2$ c. chopped pecans
$^3/_4$ c. brown sugar   1 tsp. vanilla
1 egg

Mix margarine, cream cheese, and flour together to form a soft dough. Chill for 1 hour or overnight. Roll out dough and line 30 muffin cups with dough. Mix all filling ingredients until well blended. Fill each unbaked tart shell. Bake at 350° for 15-20 minutes.

Ada Marie Miller

Easy Party Cookies

1 c. margarine $2^1/_4$ c. flour
1 c. brown sugar   1 tsp. soda
$^1/_2$ c. sugar   1 tsp. salt
2 tsp. vanilla $^1/_2$ c. M&M's
2 eggs

Cream margarine and sugar together; add vanilla and beaten eggs. Stir together; blend with creamed mixture. Add flour, soda, and salt. Mix well. Add M&M's.

Emma, Quilter

Sara's Star

We developed the Sara's Star pattern for the annual shop hop. For shop hop, twelve area quilt shops contribute a pattern 12" square. Each square is then combined to make a quilt. Daughter Ada Marie and I designed Sara's Star.

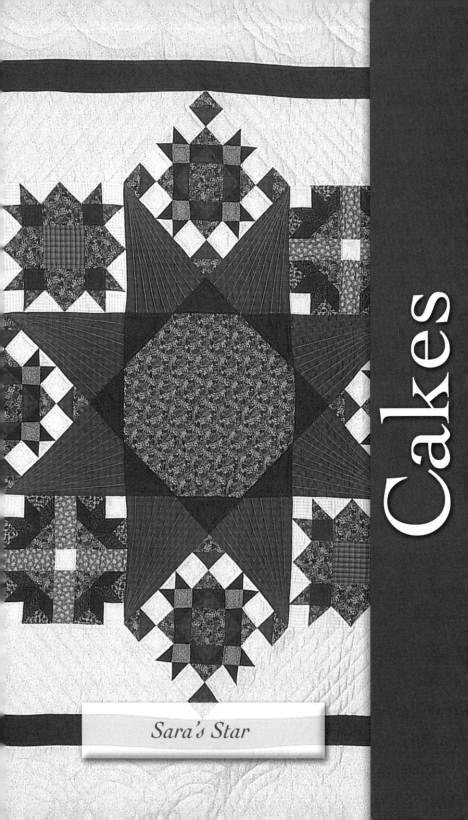

Cakes

Sara's Star

Chocolate Cake

3 c. flour	1 c. milk
2 c. sugar	1 c. boiling water
2 tsp. baking powder	1/2 c. cocoa
2 tsp. soda	1 tsp. vanilla
1/2 c. shortening	pinch salt
2 eggs	

Combine boiling water and cocoa; bring to a boil. Mix flour, sugar, baking powder, and soda. Add remaining ingredients. Bake at 350°.

Mrs. Dan C. Yoder, Quilt Piecer

Chocolate Cake

2 eggs	3 Tbsp. cocoa
3/4 c. lard or margarine	1 Tbsp. vanilla
2 c. brown sugar	2 1/2 c. flour
1/2 tsp. salt	3/4 c. boiling water
1 c. sour milk or cream	2 Tbsp. soda

Anna Zook, Quilter

Chocolate Texas Sheet Cake

1 c. margarine	1 tsp. vanilla
1 c. water	1/2 tsp. salt
4 Tbsp. cocoa	1 tsp. soda
2 c. sugar	2 eggs
2 c. flour	1/2 c. sour milk

Frosting:

1/2 c. margarine	1 lb. powdered sugar
4 Tbsp. cocoa	1 tsp. vanilla
6 Tbsp. milk	1/2 c. nuts

Melt margarine; add water and cocoa. Bring to a boil. Add remaining ingredients, stirring lightly. Bake on a cookie sheet at 350° for 20 minutes. For frosting, melt margarine, cocoa, and milk. Bring to a boil. Add remaining ingredients. Spread on cake as soon as it is out of the oven.

Mrs. James Weaver, Quilt Piecer

Texas Sheet Cake

1 c. butter	1/2 tsp. salt
1 c. water	1 tsp. soda

4 tsp. cocoa
2 c. sugar
2 c. flour

Icing:
1/2 c. butter
4 Tbsp. cocoa
6 Tbsp. milk

2 eggs, slightly beaten
1/2 c. sour cream
1 tsp. vanilla

1 lb. powdered sugar
1 c. nut meats
1 tsp. vanilla

Melt butter in saucepan. Add water and cocoa; bring to a boil. Add ingredients in order listed; stir lightly. Pour into a greased and floured cookie sheet. Bake at 350° for 15 minutes. For icing, melt butter. Add cocoa and milk; bring to a boil. Add powdered sugar, nuts, and vanilla. As soon as cake is out of the oven, spread icing on cake; cool.

Frances H. Gingerich, Quilter

Marble Cake

2 1/8 c. all-purpose flour
1 1/2 c. sugar
3 1/2 tsp. baking powder
1 tsp. salt
1/2 c. shortening
1 c. milk

1 tsp. vanilla
4 lg. egg whites
1 square baking chocolate, melted
1/4 tsp. soda
2 Tbsp. warm water
1/4 tsp. red food coloring

Sift together flour, sugar, baking powder, and salt. Add shortening, milk, and vanilla; beat for 2 minutes. Add egg whites; beat 2 minutes more. Pour 2/3 of batter into cake pan. Mix chocolate with soda and warm water. Add food coloring. Pour over white batter; cut with knife to marbelize. Bake at 350° for 25-30 minutes. Note: 3 Tbsp. cocoa plus 1/2 Tbsp. shortening may be substituted for 1 square of baking chocolate.

Mrs. Mary N. Zook, Quilter

Favorite White Layer Cake

2 1/4 c. sifted cake flour
1 1/2 c. sugar
3 1/2 tsp. baking powder
1 tsp. salt
1/2 c. shortening

1 tsp. flavoring
2/3 c. milk
1/3 c. milk
4 large egg whites
1 c. nut meats, optional

Sift together flour, sugar, baking powder, and salt. Add shortening, flavoring, and 2/3 c. milk. Beat well for 2 minutes. Add 1/3 c. milk, unbeaten egg whites, and nuts. Beat for 2 minutes. Bake in layer pans at 350° for 30-35 minutes.

Edna J. Zook, Quilter

White Cake

³/₄ c. shortening

2 c. sugar

3 c. flour

3 tsp. baking powder

³/₄ c. milk

6 egg whites, beaten

Anna Zook, Quilter

Favorite 3-Egg Cake

1¹/₂ c. sugar

³/₄ c. lard or margarine or butter

3 egg yolks

1 c. sweet milk

1 tsp. vanilla

2¹/₄ c. flour

2¹/₂ tsp. baking powder

¹/₂ tsp. salt

3 egg whites, beaten

Cream together sugar, shortening, and egg yolks. Add milk and vanilla. Stir in flour, baking powder, and salt. Add beaten egg whites. Bake.

Mrs. Mary Troyer, Quilter

Sun Gold Coconut Cake

2 c. white sugar

1 c. butter

4 egg yolks

1 tsp. vanilla

1 c. milk

pinch salt

1 c. coconut

3 c. flour

3 tsp. baking powder

4 egg whites

Topping:

1³/₄ c. sugar

³/₄ c. water

1³/₄ Tbsp. butter

¹/₄ c. light Karo

Combine ingredients in order given. Bake. For topping, combine sugar, water, butter, and Karo in a saucepan. Cook for 5 minutes. Add vanilla; stir. Spoon over warm cake.

Lizzie Yoder, Quilt Piecer

Robin Hood Sunshine Cake

8 egg whites

³/₄ tsp. cream of tartar

³/₄ tsp. salt

1 c. sugar

8 egg yolks

¹/₂ c. sugar

1 c. Robin Hood flour

2 Tbsp. cold water

1 tsp. lemon extract

1 tsp. vanilla

Beat egg whites until foamy; add cream of tartar and salt. Mix well.

Add 1 c. sugar gradually, continuing to beat until stiff peaks are formed. Set aside. Beat egg yolks until thick and light colored. Add ½ c. sugar gradually and continue to beat until fluffy. Combine water, lemon extract, and vanilla. Add flour alternately with water, beginning and ending with flour. Fold in egg white meringue. Mix slowly. Pour into an ungreased tube pan. Bake at 325° for 60 minutes.

Mrs. Andy J. Swartzentruber, Quilter

Butterscotch Sundae Cake

2¼ c. sifted Gold Medal flour	½ c. shortening
3 tsp. baking powder	1 c. milk
1 tsp. salt	1 tsp. vanilla
1¾ c. brown sugar	2 large eggs

Marshmallow Frosting:

2 egg whites	¼ tsp. cream of tartar
1½ c. sugar	¼ lb. miniature marshmallows
⅓ c. water	

Topping:

¼ c. brown sugar	3 Tbsp. water
3 Tbsp. butter	

Sift flour, baking powder, and salt into a bowl. Add sugar, shortening, milk, and vanilla. Beat for 2 minutes. Add eggs; beat for 2 minutes longer. Bake in a 9x13 pan at 350° for 35-45 minutes. For frosting, beat egg whites, sugar, water, and cream of tartar over boiling water until it stands in peaks. Add marshmallows; beat until marshmallows are melted. Spread over cake. For topping, combine ingredients and bring to a full rolling boil. Drizzle over frosting.

Clara Yoder, Quilt Marker

Pumpkin Pie Cake

1 can evaporated milk	3 eggs
2 c. pumpkin	1 yellow cake mix
1 c. sugar	¾ c. butter, melted
4 tsp. pumpkin pie spice	whipped cream

Combine evaporated milk, pumpkin, sugar, pie spice, and eggs; beat. Pour into a 9x13 pan. Sprinkle cake mix over top. Drizzle with melted butter. Bake at 350° for 50-60 minutes or until done; cool. Top with whipped cream.

Sadie Yoder, Quilt Binder

Hummingbird Cake

3^1/$_2$ c. flour
1 tsp. baking soda
1^1/$_2$ tsp. cinnamon
1^1/$_2$ c. sugar
1 c. vegetable oil
8 oz. crushed pineapple, undrained

1 tsp. salt
3 eggs, beaten
1^1/$_2$ tsp. vanilla
2 c. crushed bananas
1 c. nuts

Frosting:
8 oz. cream cheese
^{1}/$_2$ c. butter

3-4 c. powdered sugar

In a bowl, combine flour, soda, and cinnamon. Cream together oil, sugar, and vanilla. Beat until fluffy. Add eggs. Blend in dry ingredients. Add remaining ingredients and mix well. Pour into a greased 9x13 baking pan. Bake at 350° for 25-30 minutes; cool. For frosting, cream together cream cheese and butter. Add powdered sugar to reach desired consistency. Spread over cooled cake.

Sara Yoder

Carrot Cake

2 c. all-purpose flour
2 c. sugar
^{1}/$_2$ tsp. salt
1 tsp. baking soda
2 tsp. ground cinnamon
3 eggs

1^1/$_2$ c. vegetable oil
2 c. finely grated carrots
1 tsp. vanilla
1 c. crushed pineapple
coconut
1 c. chopped nuts, divided

Cream Cheese Frosting:
2 (3 oz.) pkg. cream cheese,
  softened
3 c. powdered sugar

6 Tbsp. butter or margarine
1 tsp. vanilla

In a mixing bowl, combine dry ingredients. Add eggs, oil, carrots, and vanilla; beat until combined. Stir in pineapple, coconut, and ^{1}/$_2$ c. nuts. Pour into a greased 9x13 baking pan. Bake at 350° for 50-60 minutes or until cake tests done. Cool. Combine frosting ingredients in a small bowl; mix until well blended. Frost cooled cake. Sprinkle with remaining nuts.

Ada, Quilter

Apple Cake

4 c. diced apples	2 c. flour
2 eggs	1 c. nuts
$^1/_2$ c. salad oil	$^1/_2$ tsp. salt
1 tsp. vanilla	2 tsp. soda
2 c. brown sugar	$^1/_2$ tsp. cinnamon

Glaze:

$^1/_4$ c. margarine	$^1/_2$ c. brown sugar
1 Tbsp. flour	$^1/_2$ c. milk
1 tsp. vanilla	

Beat eggs. Pour over diced apples; mix well. Add oil; mix well. Add remaining ingredients; mix. Bake at 350° for 45-55 minutes; cool. For glaze, combine ingredients and cook until thick. Pour over cake just before serving. This cake is delicious when served warm with ice cream.

Marlene Yoder, Quilt Piecer

Beet Cake

3 egg yolks	1 tsp. cinnamon
1 c. cooking oil	1 tsp. vanilla
$1^1/_2$ c. brown sugar	1 c. shredded beets
2 c. flour	1 c. shredded carrots
2 tsp. baking powder	1 c. nuts
$^1/_4$ tsp. salt	3 egg whites, beaten

Topping:

1 c. cream	$^3/_4$ c. fine coconut
1 c. brown sugar	nuts, optional

Cream together egg yolks, oil, and sugar. Mix together flour, baking powder, salt, and cinnamon. Combine vanilla, beets, carrots, and nuts; add to creamed mixture. Add dry ingredients; mix. Fold in egg whites. Bake in a tube pan or 9x13 pan at 350° for 1 hour. For topping, cook cream and brown sugar to caramel stage. Remove from heat and add coconut and nuts. Spread over hot cake and return to the oven for about 5-10 minutes.

Edna J. Zook, age 13, Quilter

Cherry Cheesecake

1 white cake mix	4 c. powdered sugar
2 (8 oz.) pkg. cream cheese, softened	2 c. whipping cream, whipped
	2 (21 oz.) cans cherry pie filling

Prepare cake mix according to directions on package. Pour into 2 greased 9x13 pans. Bake at 350° for 20 minutes; cool. Beat cream cheese and sugar until fluffy. Fold in whipped cream. Spread over each cake. Top with pie filling. Chill for 4 hours or overnight.

Ina Yoder

Cinnamon Coffee Cake

1 c. margarine	1 tsp. baking soda
2³/₄ c. brown sugar, divided	1 tsp. salt
2 tsp. vanilla	2 c. sour cream
4 eggs	2 Tbsp. cinnamon
3 c. flour	¹/₂ c. chopped walnuts, optional
2 tsp. baking powder	

Glaze: (optional)

³/₄ c. brown sugar	¹/₄ c. melted butter
¹/₂ c. sour cream	1 Tbsp. milk

Combine margarine and 2 c. brown sugar until fluffy; add vanilla. Add eggs, one at a time, beating well after each one. Add baking powder, soda, salt, and flour. Add sour cream; beat well until mixed. Spoon ¹/₃ of batter into a greased 10" tube pan. Combine cinnamon and remaining brown sugar. Sprinkle ¹/₃ over batter. Repeat layers twice. Bake at 350° for 70 minutes or until done. Cool for 10 minutes. Remove from pan to wire racks to cool completely. For glaze, cook ingredients together for 3 minutes. Add vanilla. Drizzle over cake.

Coffee Cake

1 c. milk	1 tsp. salt
¹/₂ c. margarine	2 eggs, beaten
¹/₂ c. sugar	1 pkg. yeast
3¹/₂-4 c. flour	¹/₂ c. warm water

Topping:

¹/₃ c. brown sugar	1 tsp. cinnamon
¹/₃ c. flour	¹/₂ c. nuts
3 Tbsp. butter, melted	

Filling:

3 Tbsp. flour (heaping)	1 c. sugar
1 c. milk	1 tsp. vanilla
1 c. Crisco	2^1/$_2$ c. powdered sugar

Heat milk to lukewarm. Dissolve yeast in ^{1}/$_2$ c. warm water. Cream together sugar and margarine. Add eggs, salt, yeast mixture, and milk, then flour. Let rise once. Put into three 9" cake pans. For topping, mix ingredients. Put on top of each layer; let set for 30 minutes. Bake at 375°. Cool. For filling, cook flour and milk until thick; cool. Cream together shortening and sugar; add flour mixture and vanilla. Mix well. Add powdered sugar; mix well. Split each cake and put filling between layers.

Fannie Troyer, Quilt Binder

Cherry Coffee Cake

1 c. margarine	^{1}/$_2$ tsp. almond extract
1^3/$_4$ c. sugar	3 c. flour
4 eggs	^{1}/$_2$ tsp. salt
1 tsp. vanilla	1 can cherry pie filling
1^1/$_2$ tsp. baking powder	

Cream together margarine and sugar. Add eggs, one at a time, beating well after each addition. Add vanilla, almond extract, baking powder, flour, and salt. Remove 1 c. batter. Spread remainder into a greased jellyroll pan. Spread with pie filling. Drop reserved batter on top by spoonsful. Bake at 350° for 45 minutes. Glaze when cool. Other fruit filling may be used.

Laura Yoder, Quilter

Mahogany Chiffon Cake

^{3}/$_4$ c. boiling water	^{1}/$_2$ c. cooking oil
^{1}/$_2$ c. cocoa	7 egg yolks, unbeaten
1^3/$_4$ c. flour	2 tsp. vanilla
1^3/$_4$ c. sugar	1 c. (7-8) egg whites
1^1/$_2$ tsp. soda	^{1}/$_2$ tsp. cream of tartar
1 tsp. salt	

Combine boiling water and cocoa; cool. Sift flour, sugar, soda, and salt into a bowl. Make a well and add oil, egg yolks, cocoa mixture, and vanilla. Beat until smooth. In a large bowl, beat egg whites and cream of tartar until very stiff. Pour egg yolk mixture gradually over beaten egg whites, gently folding with rubber scraper just until blended. Pour into ungreased 10" tube pan. Bake at 325° for 65-70 minutes.

Susan Miller

Angel Food Cake

1¹/₂ c. egg whites, room temp.   ¹/₂ tsp. cream of tartar
¹/₄ tsp. salt   1¹/₂ c. cake flour
1 c. white sugar   1 c. powdered sugar
1¹/₂ tsp. vanilla

Beat egg whites and salt. Gradually add remaining ingredients. Pour into a tube pan. Bake at 350° for 45 minutes.

Sara Yoder

Chocolate Angel Cake

¹/₂ c. powdered sugar   1¹/₂ tsp. cream of tartar
1 c. cake flour   ¹/₂ tsp. salt
¹/₄ c. baking cocoa   1 c. sugar
1¹/₂ c. (10) egg whites

Frosting:
1¹/₂ c. whipping cream   ¹/₂ tsp. salt
¹/₂ c. sugar   ¹/₂ tsp. vanilla
¹/₄ c. cocoa

Sift together powdered sugar, flour, and cocoa three times; set aside. Beat egg whites, cream of tartar, and salt until soft peaks form. Add sugar, 2 Tbsp. at a time, beating until stiff peaks form. Gradually fold in cocoa mixture, about a fourth at a time. Spoon into an ungreased 10" tube pan. Bake on lowest oven rack at 375° for 35-40 minutes or until the top springs back when lightly touched. Immediately invert pan; cool completely. Run a knife around edges and center tube to loosen; remove cake. For frosting, combine ingredients. Cover; chill for 1 hour. Beat until stiff peaks form. Spread over top and sides of cake. Refrigerate.

Anna Yoder, Quilter

Jellyroll

4 eggs, room temperature   1 tsp. vanilla
1 c. sugar   ³/₄ tsp. baking powder
1 c. Hi-Lite flour   ¹/₈ tsp. salt

Beat eggs until fluffy. Add sugar; beat with egg beater. Add vanilla. Add flour, baking powder, and salt. For chocolate, put 2 level Tbsp. cocoa in a cup; fill up with flour. Use a wire whip to fold in flour. Bake at 350° for 13 minutes. For chocolate, bake for 15 minutes. Cool slightly. Put on floured paper towel. Roll up.

Mattie Troyer, Quilter

Jellyroll

5 egg yolks	$^1/_4$ tsp. salt
$^3/_4$ c. sugar	1 tsp. vanilla
$^3/_4$ c. Calla Lily flour	5 egg whites
$^3/_4$ tsp. baking powder	

Filling:

7 Tbsp. flour	$1^1/_3$ c. hot water
$^2/_3$ c. brown sugar	5 Tbsp. butter

Beat egg yolks, then add sugar. Add flour, baking powder, salt, and vanilla. Beat egg whites until stiff; fold in.

Mrs. Eli D. Yoder

Sponge Roll

4 eggs, room temperature	1 c. sifted cake flour
1 tsp. vanilla	$^3/_4$ tsp. baking powder
1 c. sugar	$^1/_4$ tsp. salt

Beat eggs until light colored. For chocolate, put 2 Tbsp. cocoa in a cup and fill up with flour. Bake at 350° for 13-15 minutes.

Mrs. Ura A. Troyer, Quilter

Delicious Crumb Cake

1 c. sugar	3 tsp. baking powder
1 c. brown sugar	3 eggs, beaten
$^3/_4$ c. shortening	1 c. milk
4 c. flour	1 tsp. vanilla

Combine sugars, shortening, flour, and baking powder; mix well to make crumbs. Reserve 1 c. crumbs for top. Add remaining ingredients. Pour into a 9x13 pan. Top with reserved crumbs. Bake.

Mrs. John M. Zook, Quilter

Graham Streusel Cake

1 yellow cake mix

Crumbs:

2 c. graham cracker crumbs	$^3/_4$ c. chopped nuts
$^3/_4$ c. brown sugar	1 tsp. cinnamon
$^1/_2$ c. butter	

Mix cake mix as directed on package. Mix crumbs. Pour half of batter into a 9x13 pan; top with half of crumbs. Repeat layers. Bake. Make a glaze of powdered sugar and water; drizzle over cooled cake.

Mrs. Abe J. Yoder, Quilter

ABOUT THE QUILT
Winner's Circle

A good friend gave us the Winner's Circle pattern over 20 years ago. She told us it was a traditional pattern back then already. We've used it many times in lots of color variations over the past 20 years.

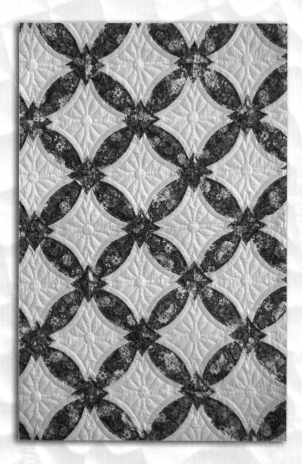

Pies

Winner's Circle

Apple Pie

4 c. shredded apples	1/2 c. water
2 c. sugar	1 tsp. lemon juice
3/4 c. water	pinch salt
2 Tbsp. fine tapioca	2 Tbsp. butter

Combine apples, sugar, and 3/4 c. water. Bring to a boil. Combine tapioca and 1/2 c. water; add to apples. Bring just to a boil. Add remaining ingredients.

Mrs. Dan Schlabach, Quilter

All-American Apple Pie

1 c. sugar	1/4 tsp. salt
2 Tbsp. flour	1 Tbsp. lemon juice
1/2 tsp. cinnamon	5 c. thinly sliced apples
1/4 tsp. nutmeg	2 Tbsp. butter

Crumbs:

1 c. flour	1/2 tsp. soda
1/2 c. brown sugar	1/4 c. margarine

Combine dry ingredients. Add apples and lemon juice. Put half of the mixture into a pastry-lined pie pan. Dot with butter and add remaining filling. Top with crumbs. Bake at 375° for 35-40 minutes. Yields 1 pie.

Mrs. James Weaver, Quilt Piecer

Apple Pie Filling

1 1/2 c. water	1 tsp. vanilla
1 c. sugar	1/4 tsp. cinnamon
3 Tbsp. clear jel	1/4 tsp. apple pie spice
2 tsp. ReaLemon juice	3 c. shredded apples

Combine water, sugar, and clear jel. Cook; add remaining ingredients. Yields 1 pie.

Linda Yoder, Quilt Piecer

Dutch Apple Pie

3 c. sliced apples   3 c. flour
1 c. brown sugar   1 tsp. cinnamon
4 Tbsp. butter or margarine   3 Tbsp. cream

Combine flour, sugar, and cinnamon. Cut in the butter with a pastry blender. Place sliced apples in an unbaked pie shell. Sprinkle crumb mixture over apples. Drizzle cream over top. Bake at 375° for 35 minutes or until apples are soft and a rich syrup has formed.

Mrs. Andy J. Swartzentruber, Quilter

Quick Snitz Pie

8 c. applesauce $^1/_2$ tsp. allspice
$1^1/_2$ tsp. cinnamon   1 c. sugar
1 tsp. cloves $^1/_2$ c. water
$^1/_2$ tsp. nutmeg $^3/_8$ c. clear jel

Combine applesauce, cinnamon, cloves, nutmeg, allspice, and sugar. Heat. Add water and clear jel. Cook, stirring constantly, for 15 minutes; cool. Make half moon pies or regular snitz pies.

Ada Marie Miller, Quilt Piecer

Pumpkin Pie

5 egg yolks $^1/_2$ tsp. allspice
5 egg whites, beaten $^1/_2$ tsp. nutmeg
$^1/_2$ c. brown sugar   2 c. pumpkin
3 Tbsp. flour (heaping)   2 cans evaporated milk
1 tsp. cinnamon   milk
$^1/_2$ tsp. cloves

Pour evaporated milk into a measuring pitcher. Add milk to make 5 cups. Combine all ingredients, folding in beaten egg whites last. Bake at 425° for 10 minutes. Reduce heat to 375° and bake until done. Yields 2 large pies.

Laura Troyer, Quilt Piecer

Pumpkin Pie

3/4 c. sugar
3/4 c. brown sugar
1 1/2 c. pumpkin (scant)
2 Tbsp. flour (scant)
1 Tbsp. butter
1 egg
2 egg yolks

2 egg whites, beaten
3 c. milk
1 c. evaporated milk
1/2 tsp. salt
1/2 tsp. cinnamon
1/2 tsp. nutmeg
1/4 tsp. allspice

Combine all ingredients, adding egg whites last. Yields 2 pies.

Miss Anna D. Hershberger, Quilt Piecer

Custard Pie

1 gal. milk
12 egg yolks
3 c. brown sugar
4 Tbsp. flour

4 Tbsp. cornstarch
2 tsp. salt
vanilla
12 egg whites, beaten until stiff

Heat milk. Mix egg yolks, brown sugar, flour, and cornstarch with a little milk, then add to hot milk. Add salt and vanilla. Fold in egg whites. Bake.

Mary N. Zook, Quilter

Custard Pie

4 c. milk, scalded
3/4 c. brown sugar
3/4 c. sugar
3 Tbsp. flour

4 eggs, separated
1/2 can sweetened condensed milk
1 tsp. vanilla

Mix egg yolks, sugars, flour, and sweetened condensed milk. Add scalded milk and vanilla. Beat egg whites until stiff. Fold in. Bake at 425° for 15 minutes. Reduce heat to 350° and bake for 20 minutes or until done. Yields 2 pies.

Sara Yoder

Union Pie

2 eggs
3 c. sugar
3 c. buttermilk
1 c. sour cream

1 tsp. soda
6 Tbsp. flour
1 c. bread crumbs

Combine and pour into 3 unbaked pie shells. Bake until brown and thickened. Yields 3 pies.

Mrs. John M. Zook, Quilter

Eggnog Pie

1 tsp. gelatin
1 Tbsp. cold water
1 c. milk
$^1/_2$ c. sugar
2 Tbsp. cornstarch

$^1/_2$ tsp. salt
eggs
1 Tbsp. butter
1 Tbsp. vanilla
$1^1/_2$ c. Rich's topping or whipped cream

Soak gelatin in cold water. Scald milk. Combine sugar, salt, and cornstarch. Mix well. Add to milk; cook until thick. Add eggs; cook a little longer. Add butter, vanilla, and gelatin. Cool, then fold in whipped cream. Pour into a baked pie shell. Let set. Add fruit filling desired. Put whipped cream on top. Yields 2 pies.

Arlene Hershberger, Quilt Piecer

Pecan Pie

3 eggs, beaten
1 c. dark Karo
$^1/_2$ c. light Karo
1 tsp. vanilla

$^1/_4$ tsp. salt
2 Tbsp. butter
1 Tbsp. flour
1 c. pecans

Mix first 6 ingredients together. Mix nuts and flour; add to first mixture. Bake at 350° for 40 minutes or a little longer. Yields 1 pie.

Mrs. Ura A. Troyer, Quilter

Pecan Pie

3 eggs	$^1/_4$ c. brown sugar
1 Tbsp. flour	pinch salt
1 c. light Karo	$^3/_4$ c. nuts
2 Tbsp. butter, melted	$^1/_4$ c. water

Mix sugar, flour, and salt with unbeaten eggs. Mix very well. Add butter, then add Karo, water, and nuts. Mix well. Bake at 450° for about 15 minutes or until nicely browned, then reduce heat to 350° until done.

Mrs. Effie Hershberger, Quilter

Pecan Pie

1 tsp. vanilla	1 c. light Karo
3 eggs	$^1/_2$ c. brown sugar
$^1/_2$ c. nuts	pinch salt
1 Tbsp. butter	$^1/_4$ c. water
1 Tbsp. flour	

Cream butter and sugar. Add beaten eggs, flour, salt, vanilla, water, and Karo. Stir well. Add nuts; bake at 350°.

Mrs. Andrew A. Yoder, Quilt Piecer

Pecan Pie

2 eggs, beaten	1 c. milk
$^1/_2$ c. sugar	1 tsp. vanilla
1 c. molasses	2 Tbsp. melted butter
1 Tbsp. flour	1 c. chopped pecans
1 Tbsp. salt	

Mix all together and pour into an unbaked pie shell. Variation: Instead of pecans, use $^1/_2$ c. quick oats and $^1/_2$ c. coconut. Yields 1 pie.

Mrs. John M. Zook, Quilter

Pecan Pie

3 eggs	$^1/_2$ c. pecans
$^1/_2$ tsp. vanilla	$^3/_4$ c. Karo
1 tsp. butter	$^3/_4$ c. sugar

Beat eggs. Add Karo, sugar, butter, and vanilla; beat again. Put into an unbaked pie shell. Bake at 300° for 50 minutes.

Verna H. Gingerich, Quilter

Praline Pecan Pie

$^1/_3$ c. brown sugar
$^1/_3$ c. butter
$^1/_2$ c. chopped pecans
$1^1/_3$ c. milk

1 pkg. vanilla, butterscotch, or
   butter pecan instant pudding
2 c. Cool Whip

Mix brown sugar, butter, and pecans together. Bring to a boil. Cool slightly, then put into a baked pie shell. Mix pudding and milk; let set. Add Cool Whip. Spread on top of pecan mixture.

Linda Yoder, Quilt Piecer

Sour Cream Pecan Pie

1 unbaked pastry shell
$^1/_2$ c. sour cream
1 c. sugar
1 tsp. vanilla
$1^1/_4$ c. pecans

3 eggs, beaten
$^1/_2$ c. light Karo
2 Tbsp. butter, melted
$^1/_8$ tsp. salt

Bake at 350° until filling is slightly puffy. This pie is not so sweet.

Freda Miller

Mock Pecan Pie

$^1/_4$ c. butter
$^1/_2$ c. sugar
1 c. dark Karo
$^1/_2$ c. coconut

$^1/_2$ c. water
$^1/_2$ tsp. salt
3 eggs, beaten
$^1/_2$ c. quick oats

Cream butter to soften. Add sugar and Karo; beat well. Add eggs, salt, and water. Stir in oats and coconut. Bake at 300° for 50 minutes.

Oatmeal Pie

7 eggs
3 c. milk
2 c. Karo or pancake syrup
$1^1/_2$ c. oatmeal
2 c. sugar

$^1/_2$ c. butter, melted
1 Tbsp. flour
salt
1 c. nuts

Beat eggs, then add sugar and Karo; beat well. Add remaining ingredients. Bake at 450° for 15 minutes. Reduce heat to 350° and bake until done. Yields 3 pies.

Anna Yoder, Quilter

Strawberry Pie

1 pkg. strawberry Jell-O
1½ c. hot water
¼ c. sugar

pinch salt
2 c. crushed strawberries
1 c. whipped cream

Dissolve Jell-O in hot water. Add sugar and salt. Chill until slightly thickened. Add strawberries. Fold in whipped cream. Put into a baked pie shell. Chill.

Mattie Hershberger, Quilter

Rhubarb Custard Pie

4½ c. sugar
6 Tbsp. flour
12 Tbsp. evaporated milk

5 eggs, beaten
6 c. diced rhubarb

Mix; pour into an unbaked pie shell. Bake at 425° for 12 minutes. Reduce heat to 325°; bake for 40 minutes or until done. Yields 3 pies.

Laura Yoder, Quilter

French Rhubarb Pie

1 egg, beaten
1 c. sugar
2 Tbsp. flour

2 c. diced rhubarb
½ tsp. vanilla

Topping:
¾ c. flour
½ c. brown sugar

⅓ c. melted butter

Mix together and put into an unbaked pie shell. Mix crumbs; put on top of filling. Bake.

Note: a bit of orange flavoring makes it more tasty. Even a sprinkle of Jell-O or Tang will do.

Mrs. John E. Weaver

Rhubarb Custard Pie

1 c. sugar	2 egg yolks
2 Tbsp. flour	1¼ c. evaporated milk or half-and-half
4 Tbsp. butter	2½ c. rhubarb

Add enough water to sugar and flour to make a paste. Add egg yolks, butter, and milk. Add diced rhubarb. Pour into an unbaked pie shell. Bake at 425° for 12 minutes. Reduce heat to 325° and bake for 40 minutes longer. When almost done, beat egg whites until stiff, then add sugar; beat slightly. Put on top of pie and bake until nice and brown.

Mrs. Junior Weaver, Quilt Marker

Rhubarb Cream Pie

6 Tbsp. butter	1½ c. sugar
6 c. chopped rhubarb	6 Tbsp. cornstarch
1½ water	6 egg yolks, beaten
3 c. sugar	¾ c. evaporated milk

Melt butter; add rhubarb, water, and sugar. Cook until tender. Combine remaining ingredients. Add this to cooked rhubarb. Cook until thick. Put into 2 baked pie shells. Top with whipped topping. Yields 2 pies.

Mrs. Dan C. Yoder, Quilt Piecer

Cream Pie Filling

4 c. milk	vanilla
1 c. sugar	salt
⅓ c. cornstarch (heaping)	¼ c. butter
3 egg yolks	

Heat milk. Mix sugar and cornstarch with a little milk. Add egg yolks. Add mixture to milk. When thickened, add butter, vanilla, and salt. For chocolate pie, add ⅓ c. cocoa. This can be used for raisin, coconut cream, and peanut butter pie. Yields 2 pies. For Oreo pudding, make two batches.

Esther Hershberger, Quilter

Raisin Cream Pie

³/₄ c. raisins	¹/₄ c. powdered sugar
2 Tbsp. brown sugar	1 pkg. instant vanilla pudding
water	³/₄ c. milk
8 oz. cream cheese	1 c. Rich's topping, whipped

Cook raisins and sugar in a little water for 10 minutes over low heat; cool. Mix cream cheese and powdered sugar until creamy. Whip pudding and milk together. Mix all ingredients together, reserving some topping for the top. Very good. Yields 1 pie.

Mrs. Ella Keim, Quilt Piecer

Raisin Cream Pie

4 c. raisins	12 Tbsp. flour or cornstarch
10 c. water	4 c. rich milk
4 c. brown sugar	4 Tbsp. butter
8 egg yolks	vanilla
3 c. sugar	

Cook raisins, water, and brown sugar for 10 minutes. Add egg yolks, sugar, flour, and milk. When cooked, add butter and vanilla. Fill pie shells; top with whipped cream. Yields 6 pies.

Sara Yoder

Raisin Crumb Pie

1 c. raisins	2 c. water
³/₄ c. brown sugar	¹/₂ tsp. salt
2 Tbsp. cornstarch	1 Tbsp. vinegar

Crumbs:

³/₄ c. flour	¹/₂ c. brown sugar
¹/₄ c. quick oats	¹/₂ tsp. soda
¹/₄ c. margarine	

Combine ingredients in a saucepan. Cook until thickened; cool. Put into an unbaked pie shell. Mix crumbs and put on top. Bake. Yields 1 pie.

Mrs. John M. Zook, Quilter

Baked Butterscotch Pie

2 Tbsp. flour	1 ¹/₂ hot milk
2 Tbsp. butter	2 eggs, separated
1 c. brown sugar	vanilla

Cream together butter and flour. Mix egg yolks and brown sugar; add to butter mixture. Add hot milk and vanilla. Beat egg whites until fluffy, but not too stiff; fold in. Bake at 350° for 45 minutes. Yields 1 large pie.

Mrs. Mary Troyer, Quilter

Peanut Butter Pie

1 baked pie shell	¹/₂ c. peanut butter
1 c. powdered sugar	1 lg. pkg. vanilla pudding

Meringue:

3 egg whites	¹/₄ tsp. cream of tartar
¹/₂ c. sugar	1 tsp. cornstarch

Mix together powdered sugar and peanut butter. Sprinkle ²/₃ of mixture over baked pie shell. Make the pudding according to package directions. Cool and pour over mixture. For meringue, beat egg whites until foamy. Mix together sugar, cream of tartar, and cornstarch. Add to egg whites. Beat until stiff. Spread on top of pie. Sprinkle with remaining crumbs. Bake at 350° for 15 minutes.

Emma, Quilter

Lemon Sponge Pie

2 Tbsp. butter	¹/₂ tsp. salt
1 c. sugar	1¹/₄ c. hot milk
3 eggs, separated	2 Tbsp. flour
¹/₂ c. lemon juice	¹/₂ tsp. lemon rind

Cream butter; add sugar and egg yolks. Beat until light and fluffy. Stir in flour, salt, lemon juice, lemon rind, and milk. Fold in stiffly beaten egg whites. Bake at 400° for 10 minutes. Reduce heat to 350° and bake until set. Yields 1 pie.

Clara Yoder, Quilt Marker

Lemon Pie

1 pkg. lemon Jell-O
1/2 c. sugar
1 c. whipped topping

1 c. boiling water
1 Tbsp. ReaLemon juice

Mix Jell-O, boiling water, sugar, and lemon juice. When starting to thicken, add topping.

Mrs. Nelson E. Weaver

Chocolate Angel Strata Pie

2 egg whites
1/4 tsp. salt
1/8 tsp. cinnamon, optional

1/2 c. sugar
1/2 tsp. vinegar

Chocolate Cream Filling:
2 egg yolks, slightly beaten
3/4 c. semisweet chocolate chips, melted

1 c. Rich's topping
1/4 c. water
1/8 tsp. cinnamon, optional

Beat egg whites with vinegar, cinnamon, and salt. Add sugar. Spread on bottom and up sides of unbaked pie shell. Bake at 350° for 15-18 minutes or until done. This usually is puffed up, but will go down. I usually put unbaked pie shell in toaster to brown before I put egg whites in. For chocolate filling, add egg yolks and water to melted chocolate chips. Spread 3 Tbsp. over pie shell and egg whites. Chill remainder. Beat topping and cinnamon until very thick. Spread half over chocolate. Combine remaining topping with chocolate mixture. Spread over topping layer. Put dollops of topping on top if desired. Chill for 4 hours.

Freda Miller, Quilt Piecer · Katy Yoder, Quilt Piecer

Oreo Pie

3 pkg. instant vanilla pudding
4 1/2 c. milk
2 (8 oz.) pkg. cream cheese

2 (8 oz.) cartons Cool Whip
2 c. powdered sugar
32 Oreo cookies, crushed

Mix pudding and milk; let set until thick. Cream together cream cheese, Cool Whip, and powdered sugar, and add cookie crumbs. Mix with pudding. Pour into a baked pie shell. Top with Cool Whip. Yields 4 pies.

Ada Marie Miller, Quilt Piecer

Rice Krispie Pie

3 eggs
$^1/_4$ tsp. salt
1 tsp. vanilla
1 c. Rice Krispies

$^1/_2$ c. brown sugar
1 c. light Karo
2 Tbsp. butter

Beat eggs; add remaining ingredients. Pour into an unbaked pie shell. Bake at 350°. Yields 1 pie.

Fannie Yoder, Quilter

Rice Krispie Pie

2 eggs
$^2/_3$ c. sugar
$^1/_2$ c. Karo
$^1/_4$ tsp. salt

1 tsp. vanilla
3 Tbsp. butter, melted
$^1/_4$ c. water
$1^1/_4$ c. Rice Krispies

Beat eggs; add sugar, Karo, salt, vanilla, butter, and water. Fold in Rice Krispies. Pour into an unbaked pie shell. Bake at 375° for 35-40 minutes.

Iva Gingerich, Quilter

Fry Pies

9 c. cake flour
3 c. Creamtex or B&B shortening
1 Tbsp. salt

2 c. water
2 Tbsp. sugar

Roll dough out thin and cut into desired shape and size. (I use a Lifetime coffeepot lid to cut a circle.) Fill with pie filling. Fry in B&B shortening from the bulk food store. Glaze with a thin powdered sugar and water glaze.

Ada Marie Miller, Quilt Piecer

Best Pie Crust

1½ c. lard	1 Tbsp. vinegar
½ c. milk	1 tsp. baking powder
1 egg	1 tsp. salt
1 Tbsp. brown sugar	4 c. flour

Combine all ingredients except flour. Add flour gradually until mixed with spoon. So easy and delicious!

Linda Yoder, Quilt Piecer

Pie Crust

6 c. flour	1 egg
2 c. lard	1 tsp. vinegar
½ tsp. salt	water

Blend together flour, lard, and salt to make coarse crumbs. In a cup, combine egg and vinegar, beaten together. Add water to fill the cup. Combine all ingredients with a fork.

Mrs. Malinda Miller, Quilt Marker

a Stitch in Time

There's hope if you find grease marks on fabric. Shampoo for oily hair will often remove the stain.

Before washing fabric, use the serger sewing machine to stitch the edges of your material to prevent fraying.

The Quilt

Quilts are a family heirloom
With plain and printed colors.
There's Alabama Star, Log Cabin,
Rubic's Cube, and many others.

There's also one called Tree of Life,
And Amish Shadow, too.
Trail of Stars and Dresden Plate,
Just to name a few.

The work that goes into a quilt
As piece by piece you cut,
And then you sew together
All the pieces that you've got.

With happiness you put in frame
The prize you labored for;
As you sit down and stitch in love
You quilt and stitch some more.

Love Around the World

Love Around the World is an interesting quilt. I used the Country Love pattern for the appliquéing part. Then I tried to match all the fabrics used in the Trip Around the World quilt. Toward the outer border, I added more squares to complement the border with the same shades of fabric. Today the world needs more Love Around the World, doesn't it?

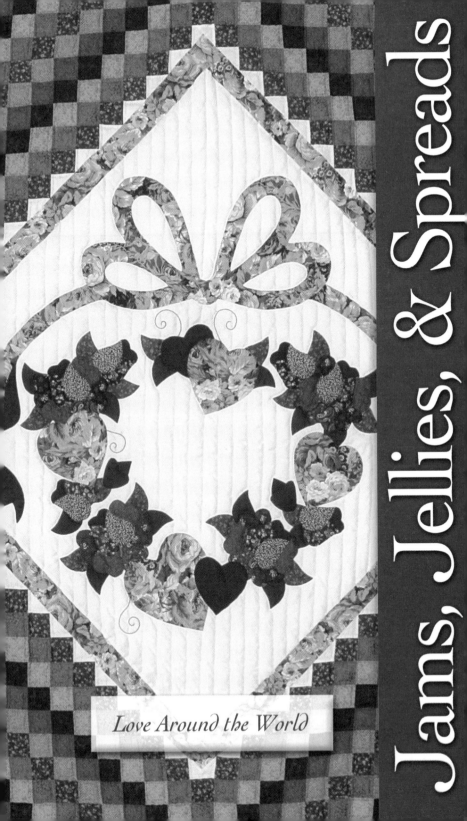

Jams, Jellies, & Spreads

Love Around the World

Strawberry Jam

2 c. crushed strawberries
4 c. sugar

$^3/_4$ c. water
$^1/_3$ c. + 1 Tbsp. fruit pectin

Mix strawberries and sugar; let set 10 minutes. Combine water and pectin; cook for 1 minute. Stir in strawberries. Cook for 3 minutes. Put into containers. Let set 24 hours. Freeze.

Sara Yoder

Strawberry Jam

2 c. crushed strawberries
4 c. sugar

1 pkg. Sure-Jell
$^2/_3$ c. water

Mix Sure-Jell and water. Put berries in a saucepan and heat to almost boiling, then add Sure-Jell. Bring to a rolling boil. Remove from heat. Immediately add sugar. Pour into cans; freeze.

Ada Marie Miller

Peanut Butter Spread

10 c. brown sugar
5 c. boiling water
$^3/_4$ c. Karo

5-6 lb. peanut butter
2-3 qt. marshmallow crème

Bring brown sugar, boiling water, and Karo to a boil; cool. Add remaining ingredients. Makes a fix-n-mix bowl full. Finger-lickin' good!

Freida Yoder, Quilter · Freda Miller

Peanut Butter

1 c. brown sugar
1 c. water
2 egg whites
$^1/_2$ c. sugar

$^1/_4$ c. Karo
$1^1/_2$ c. peanut butter
$^1/_2$ tsp. maple flavoring

Combine brown sugar and water; bring to a boil and cook for one minute. Set aside to cool. In a double boiler, mix together egg whites, sugar, and Karo. Beat with egg beater until fluffy; cool. Add peanut butter to second cooled mixture. Add to first mixture. Add flavoring. Enjoy!

Sara Yoder

Sugar Spread

2 c. sugar	3 marshmallows
2 c. light Karo	1/4 c. water

Bring this to a full boil; cool slightly. Beat whites of 2 eggs until stiff. Pour syrup over white of eggs slowly, and keep on stirring until cold. Add maple flavoring to suit your taste. Very good.

Mrs. Ella Keim, Quilt Piecer

Apple Butter

2 gal. cider	4 c. sugar
5-6 qt. applesauce	spices

Cook only in a copper or stainless steel kettle.

Sara Yoder

a Stitch in Time

White fabric or paper behind the eye of a needle makes it easier to see when threading it.

To mark, using a template, begin marking at one corner and proceed to the middle and then begin at the opposite corner and mark to the middle again to prevent stretching.

ABOUT THE QUILT
Peace at the Ocean

Our daughter, Ada Marie, likes challenging quilts, which is what her Peace at the Ocean is. She started with the Mariners' Compass, then added the ocean theme by using the Ocean Wave pattern. To complete the quilt, she added birds in the corners so they can watch over the captain as he guides the ship.

Snacks

Peace at the Ocean

Snack

3 Tbsp. sour cream &   1 lb. Ritz crackers
  onion powder   1 c. Mazola oil
  Mix together; put in a loaf pan. Bake at 250° for 20 minutes.

Miss Anna D. Hershberger, Piecer

Ranch Pretzels

2 lb. pretzels   ½ tsp. garlic powder
¾ c. Crisco oil   ½ tsp. lemon pepper
1 pkg. Hidden Valley Ranch mix ½ tsp. dill weed
  Mix oil and seasonings; pour over pretzels. Bake at 325° for 20 minutes. Stir a
few times while baking.   *Ada Marie Miller*

Soft Pretzels

2½ c. warm water   3 Tbsp. yeast
¾ c. brown sugar   1 tsp. salt
7-8 c. bread flour
  Let rise a little. Shape into twists. Dissolve 2 Tbsp. soda in 1 c. warm water. Dip
pretzels into soda water. Put on towel until dripped off, then put onto a cookie
sheet. Sprinkle lightly with pretzel salt. Let rise again. Bake until nice and brown.
Brush lightly with melted butter.   *Effie Miller, Quilter*

Cheesy Soft Pretzels

1½ c. all-purpose flour   2 Tbsp. cold butter
½ c. shredded cheddar cheese   ⅔ c. milk
2 tsp. baking powder   1 egg, beaten
1 Tbsp. brown sugar   coarse salt
¾ tsp. salt
  In a bowl, combine cheese, baking powder, sugar, and salt. Cut in butter until
crumbly. Stir in milk just until moistened. Knead on a floured surface for 1 minute.
Divide in half. Roll each portion into a 12"x8" rectangle. Cut into 8" long strips.
Fold strips in half, pinching the edges, and twist into pretzel shapes. Place on
greased baking sheets. Brush with egg; sprinkle with coarse salt. Bake at 400° for
12-15 minutes or until golden brown. Serve immediately. Yields 1½ doz. pretzels.

Lucinda Yoder, Quilt Appliqués

Simple Caramels

1 lb. brown sugar   1 can sweetened condensed milk
1 c. light Karo   1 cup butter
  Cook for 12 minutes, stirring constantly. Pour into a greased pan; cool, cut, and
wrap. If desired, pecans can be put on top or chopped pecans may be stirred in
and then pieces dipped in chocolate.   *Mrs. Abe Byler, Quilter*

Pizza Snack

Place Town House crackers on a pizza pan. Top each cracker with a half slice of pepperoni, a dab of pizza sauce, and cheese. Place in oven until cheese is melted. Eat while hot.   *Sadie Yoder, Quilt Binder*

Texas Jack

1 c. cream
1 c. sugar
1 c. light corn syrup
5 c. corn flakes

1 c. chopped nuts
2 c. Rice Krispies
1 c. coconut

In a saucepan, combine sugar, cream, and syrup. Cook over low heat to a soft ball stage. Pour mixture over the remaining ingredients. Mix all together and flatten out in pans. Cut into squares.   *Verna H. Gingerich, Quilter*

Cream Puffs

$^1/_2$ c. water
$^1/_4$ c. margarine

$^1/_2$ c. flour
2 eggs

Filling:
1 env. Dream Whip
1 pkg. instant vanilla pudding

2 c. milk
1 tsp. vanilla

Heat oven to 400°. Heat water and margarine to a rolling boil in a saucepan. Stir in flour. Stir vigorously over low heat until mixture forms a ball, about 1 minute; remove from heat. Beat in eggs all at once. Continue beating until smooth. Drop dough by $^1/_4$ c. about 3" apart onto ungreased cookie sheet. Bake until puffed and golden, 30-45 minutes. Cool. Cut off tops; pull out any soft dough. Fill with filling and replace tops; sprinkle with powdered sugar.   *Mrs. Christ Miller*

Clark Bars

1 c. margarine
$2^1/_2$ c. powdered sugar
1 (1 lb.) box graham crackers, crushed

1 c. crunchy peanut butter
3 tsp. vanilla

Mix ingredients with hands. Shape into bonbon-sized balls and dip in chocolate or coconut.

Hickory Nut Caramels

1 c. sugar
1 c. light Karo
$^2/_3$ c. cream, divided

1 Tbsp. butter
pinch salt

Cook sugar, Karo, and $^1/_3$ c. cream to soft ball stage. Add remaining cream and butter; cook to 244°. Pour over chopped nuts in a buttered pan. Cool. Cut and wrap in waxed paper.   *Frances H. Gingerich, Quilter*

Lone Star

We started our shop with this Lone Star quilt, hence our name. Its been an all-around favorite for years and continues to draw the attention of quilt lovers everywhere. I like the challenge of piecing the Lone Star, to make the diamonds meet in the corner. The corners are quilted with a feathered heart. We also put the diamonds in the border to bring more color and dimension to the quilt.

Lone Star

Miscellaneous

Hamburger Pickles

1 gal. cucumbers, thinly sliced	6 c. sugar
1 c. salt	1 Tbsp. whole cloves
1 gal. water	1 Tbsp. allspice
1 Tbsp. alum	1 Tbsp. celery seed
2 c. vinegar	1 Tbsp. stick cinnamon
2 c. water	1 tsp. turmeric

Mix salt and 1 gal. water. Put in a crock; add cucumbers. Cover crock with a cloth and a plate; soak for 3-5 days. Drain; wash in cold water. Cook for 10 minutes with 1 Tbsp. alum in enough water to cover cucumbers. Wash again. Combine vinegar, water, and sugar. Put spices in a cloth bag. Add cucumbers to vinegar mixture; add spice bag. Cook until the cucumbers look clear. Process in boiling-water bath.

Mrs. Effie Hershberger, Quilter

Refrigerator Pickles

6 c. sliced cucumbers	1 c. sliced onions
1 c. sliced green peppers	1 c. vinegar
1 tsp. celery seed	2 c. sugar
1 Tbsp. salt	

Mix all together and store in refrigerator or freezer. Do not cook anything. Ready to eat in 24 hours.

Mrs. Abe J. Yoder, Quilter

Sweet Garlic Dill Pickles

3 c. sugar	1 c. vinegar
2 Tbsp. salt	3 c. water

Slice med. cucumbers 1/4" thick into quart jars. Put 1 garlic clove and 1 dill head or 1 tsp. dill seed on top. Pour syrup over top. Put jars in canner; fill canner with water to top of jars. Process in boiling-water bath. Turn off heat. Remove lid of canner and let jars set until cool. Will be ready to eat in 2 weeks.

Mrs. Floyd Yoder

Relish

6 lg. cucumbers	2 c. vinegar
6 lg. onions	1 tsp. mustard seed

6 lg. red peppers, optional 2 tsp. celery seed
5 c. sugar 2 Tbsp. salt

Grind together cucumbers, onions, and peppers. Pour boiling water over top; let set for 30 minutes. Drain. Make vinegar solution; heat to melt sugar. Mix all together and cook for 30 minutes. Put into jars; seal.

Anna Yoder, Quilter

Green Tomato Relish

24 green tomatoes 6 c. sugar
6 green peppers 2 Tbsp. salt
12 onions 2 c. vinegar
1 red pepper $^1/_2$ c. pickling spice

Grind together tomatoes, peppers, onions, and red pepper; drain. Mix sugar, salt, and vinegar. Tie up pickling spice in a bag. Mix all together and cook for 20 minutes. Remove spice bag. Put into jars; seal.

Mrs. Dan Schlabach, Quilter

Ketchup

4 qt. tomatoes, mashed 2 c. sugar
1 Tbsp. cinnamon 1 Tbsp. pickling spice
2 Tbsp. salt 1 tsp. ground mustard
$^1/_2$ tsp. red pepper $^1/_2$ c. vinegar
1 med. onion, chopped

Mix all together; cook for 1 hour. Strain; bring to a boil again. Thicken with 4 Tbsp. cornstarch moistened with vinegar. Cook for 10 minutes, stirring constantly. Put into jars; seal. Yields about 8 pints.

Amanda Yoder, Quilter

To Can Ground Beef

15 lb. ground beef 1 c. oatmeal
$^1/_4$ c. salt 3 c. water
4 slices bread 4 eggs
36 soda crackers

Mix ingredients together. Shape into balls; put into jars. Process in boiling-water bath for 3 hours.

Mrs. Ella Keim, Quilt Piecer

Yogurt

8 c. milk	1 c. sugar
1 Tbsp. gelatin	2 Tbsp. plain yogurt
1/2 c. cold water	fruit filling, Jell-O, or flavoring

Heat milk to 190°. Cool to 130°. Soak gelatin in cold water. Add sugar and plain yogurt. Add to milk. Let set 8 hours or overnight in a warm place. Cool. Whip; add fruit filling, Jell-O, or flavoring. Save at least 2 Tbsp. plain yogurt for your next batch.

Amanda Yoder, Quilter

Dip for Fresh Fruit

8 oz. cream cheese	1 (7 oz.) jar marshmallow crème

Mix until light and fluffy. Serve with any kind of fresh fruit.

Lucinda Yoder

Fruit Cocktail to Can

2 gal. pears	1 gal. pineapple
2 1/2 gal. peaches	3 lb. green grapes
3 c. light Karo	14 c. sugar

Process in boiling-water bath for 10 minutes. This makes a big batch.

Mrs. Nelson E. Weaver, Quilter

Slush Punch

13 c. water	3 Tbsp. lemon juice
3 pkg. pineapple Jell-O	2 cans frozen orange juice concentrate
4 c. sugar	2 qt. 7-Up

Bring sugar and 4 c. water to a boil. Add remaining ingredients except 7-Up. Freeze. Remove from freezer 1 1/2 hours before serving. Put some slush into a cup, then fill with 7-Up.

Freda Miller

Rhubarb Punch

8 c. diced rhubarb	2 Tbsp. strawberry Jell-O or
2 c. hot water	1 pkg. Kool-Aid
2 c. pineapple juice	1/2 c. ReaLemon
2 1/4 c. sugar	

Put rhubarb in pan and cover with water. Cook for 10 minutes. Drain for 1 hour, reserving juice. Mix 8 c. juice with sugar. Dissolve Jell-O in hot water, pineapple juice, and ReaLemon. Add to juice. Put into jars; process in boiling-water bath for 15 minutes. When ready to serve, mix 2 liters 7-Up with 2 qt. juice.

Nettie Yoder, Quilter

Dandelion Wine

1 gal. dandelion blossoms   1 lemon
1 gal. boiling water   3 oranges, peeled
4 lb. sugar   2 Tbsp. yeast

Pour boiling water over dandelion blossoms. Let set for 3 days. Put on stove and simmer for 15 minutes. Add sugar. When warm, add lemon, oranges, and yeast. Let set for 1 week. Strain; bottle.

Play Dough

$^1/_2$ c. salt   1 c. water
1 c. flour   1 Tbsp. vegetable oil
2 Tbsp. cream of tartar   food coloring

Mix dry ingredients in saucepan. Add water and oil; stir well. Add coloring; cook over low heat, stirring constantly, until mixture gets rubbery. Turn dough onto table and knead with hands. Store in tight containers.

Sara Yoder

Homemade Baby Wipes

2 c. boiled water   Bounty paper towels
2 squirts baby bath or shampoo   1 c. rubbing alcohol

Cut roll of paper towels through the middle. Remove cardboard and put towels into an empty baby wipe can. Start it out of the middle. Add liquid; turn upside down. Or fold them and put them into a square container. Good luck!

Mrs. Nelson E. Weaver, Quilter

Plant Food

1 tsp. baking powder
1/2 tsp. ammonia
1 tsp. saltpeter

1 Tbsp. Epsom salts
1 gal. water

Water plants with this once a month, and watch your flowers grow.

Mrs. Effie Hershberger, Quilter

Pantry Plant Food

1 tsp. baking powder
1 tsp. Epsom salts
1/2 tsp. household ammonia

1 tsp. saltpeter
1 gal. lukewarm water

Give this to plants instead of their regular watering every 4-6 weeks. This perks up houseplants, especially vines and ivies.

Instead of Spraying Trees

50 lb. wood ashes
25 lb. lime

12 lb. sulphur
6 lb. coarse salt

Put this mixture around and under trees as far out around as the branches. You don't need to spray trees if this is used. For fruit trees, grapevines, raspberries, etc.

Fast Relief for Boils

Apply Vaseline to the boil, then slice a juicy lemon and put 1 slice on the affected spot. Remove this every day and put a fresh slice on until it's gone. This usually takes 3 days.

Mrs. Effie Hershberger, Quilter

a Stitch in Time

To store an old quilt, use a prewashed, white pillowcase.

Equivalents & Substitutions

3 tsp.	1 Tbsp.
4 Tbsp.	$^1/_4$ cup
2 cups	1 pint
1 lb. butter	2 c. butter
1 lb. granulated sugar	2 c. granulated sugar
1 lb. powdered sugar	$3^1/_2$ cups powdered sugar
1 lb. flour	4 c. flour
1 square chocolate	1 oz. chocolate
butter the size of an egg	$^1/_4$ c. butter
8-10 egg whites	1 c. egg whites
12-14 egg yolks	1 c. egg yolks
1 Tbsp. cornstarch	2 Tbsp. flour
1 c. sour milk	$1^1/_2$ Tbsp. lemon juice plus sweet milk to make 1 cup
1 c. molasses	1 c. sugar
1 c. honey	$^3/_4$ c. sugar plus $^1/_4$ c. liquid
1 tsp. baking powder	$^1/_4$ tsp. soda plus $^1/_2$ tsp. cream of tartar
1 lb. cornmeal	3 cups cornmeal
23 soda crackers	1 c. crumbs
15 graham crackers	1 c. crumbs
8 oz. can	1 cup
picnic can	$1^1/_4$ cups
#300 can	$1^3/_4$ cups
#1 tall can	2 cups
#303 can	2 cups
#2 can	$2^1/_2$ cups
#$2^1/_2$ can	$3^1/_2$ cups
#3 can	4 cups
#10 can	12-13 cups

Oven Temperatures

Slow	300°
Slow moderate	325°
Moderate	350°
Quick moderate	375°
Moderately hot	400°
Hot	425°
Very hot	475°

ABOUT THE QUILT
Star Spin

The Star Spin is a favorite with many people,
but it's complicated to piece. Don't try it if you're
a beginner. It takes eight fabrics of one shade and
eight of another.

Index

Star Spin

Cooking with the Horse & Buggy People

Sharing a Second Serving of Favorites
from 207 Amish Women of Holmes County, Ohio

Henry and Amanda Mast, authors and compilers of *Cooking with the Horse and Buggy People Volume II* (as well as Volume I), live close to Charm, Ohio. Their home place is in the heart of the world's largest Amish community. The Masts and their friends worked countless hours in the kitchen to perfect the 600 recipes they chose to share with you.

Good food. Laughter. Compliments. Memories. That's what this new volume of *Cooking with the Horse and Buggy People* is about.

$10.95

· 5¹/₂" x 8¹/₂" · 320 pp · Spiral Bound · Extra-Heavy Laminated Cover
· ISBN 1-890050-62-8

VOLUME I

Cooking with the Horse & Buggy People

A Collection of Over 600 Favorite Recipes from the Heart of Holmes County

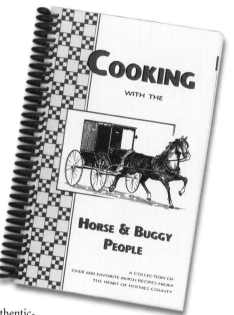

From mouth watering Amish style main dishes to kitchen dream desserts, this one has it all. Over 600 made-from-scratch recipes that please the appetite and are easy on the food budget. You'll get a whole section on canning and food preparation. The Amish, long known for their originality in the kitchen, share their favorites with you. If you desire originality, if you respect authenticity, if the Amish style cooking satisfies your taste palate—**Cooking With The Horse & Buggy People** is for you.

Contains 14 Complete Sections:
Breads, Cakes, Cookies, Desserts, Pies, Salads, Main Dishes, Soups, Cereal, Candy, Miscellaneous, Drinks, Canning, Home Remedies & Preparing Wild Game, Index.

$10.95
· 5$^{1}/_{2}$" x 8$^{1}/_{2}$" · 275 pp · Spiral Bound · Laminated Cover
· Convenient Thumb Index · ISBN 1-890050-16-4

In Its 22nd Printing, Over 140,000 sold!

Mary Yoder's Candy & Confections Cookbook

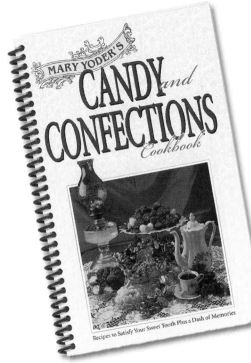

Mary Yoder

Ready for a really special treat ...one that will satisfy your sweet tooth? Dripping chocolates, dreamy fudges, reach-for-more mints, and over 100 other sweet secrets—the homemade way. Mary has over 30 years' experience in making candy and confections—for her family as well as commercially. In this book she shares her own secret recipes, never before published.

Mary Yoder's Candy and Confections Cookbook is even more! Take a good look, for example, at the 24 color photos of the author's childhood memories and unique hobbies. You'll enjoy a walk down memory lane with her through the photos of her home, gardens, and hobbies. 70 illustrations in her own original pencil art are scattered throughout the book.

The next time you need a treat so special, so unique, so mouthwatering that it can't be bought, reach for Mary Yoder's Candy and Confections Cookbook. You'll add that personal touch that's just right.

You'll make that special moment even sweeter!

$9.95

· 5¹/₂" x 8¹/₂" · 126 pp · Spiral Bound · 24 Color Photographs
· 70 Original Pencil Illustrations by Mary Yoder · ISBN 1-890050-36-9

AUTHENTIC AMISH COOKING

The Wooden Spoon
Cookbook

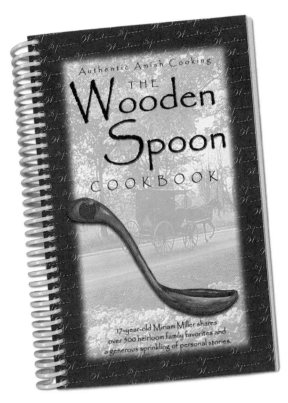

M eet 17-year-old Miriam Miller in the Wooden Spoon Cookbook. In
addition to sharing her own, her mother's, and her grandmother's
favorite recipes, Miriam shares childhood memories, stories, and personal
details of her life as a young Amish girl.

$10.95

· 5$^{1}/_{2}$" x 8$^{1}/_{2}$" · 194 pp · Spiral bound · Laminated cover · Double indexed
· ISBN 1-890050-41-5

Amish Quilting Cookbook's Annual

Quilt Giveaway!

ENTRY FORM

Name _____

Address _____

City _____ State _____ Zip _____

Phone (opt.) _____ Fax (opt.) _____

I bought Amish Quilting Cookbook at:

Name of Store _____

City _____ State _____

— Drawing held in October annually

— Sales receipt *must* accompany entry form

— No photocopies of entry form

Send to:

 Carlisle Press
2673 TR 421 · Sugarcreek, OH 44681